E243 Inclus█████████████████om each other

# Listening to Others

**BOOK 3**

BIb ID 427141

This book forms part of The Open University course E243 **Inclusive Education: learning from each other**. The complete list of books and units is as follows:

## Readers

Nind, M., Rix, J., Sheehy, K. and Simmons, K. (eds) (2003) Inclusive Education: diverse perspectives, London, David Fulton in association with The Open University (**Reader 1**).

Nind, M., Sheehy, K. and Simmons, K. (eds) (2003) Inclusive Education: learners and learning contexts, London, David Fulton in association with The Open University (**Reader 2**).

# Listening to others

**BOOK 3   Units 5 — 8**

The Open University

**Education and Language Studies
Level 2**

This publication forms part of an Open University course **E243 Inclusive Education: learning from each other**. Details of this and other Open University courses can be obtained from the Course Information and Advice Centre, PO Box 724, The Open University, Milton Keynes MK7 6ZS, United Kingdom: tel. +44 (0)1908 653231, e mail general-enquiries@open.ac.uk

Alternatively, you may visit the Open University website at http:// www.open.ac.uk where you can learn more about the wide range of courses and packs offered at all levels by The Open University.

To purchase a selection of Open University course materials visit the webshop at http://www.ouw.co.uk, or contact Open University Worldwide, Michael Young Building, Walton Hall, Milton Keynes MK7 6AA, United Kingdom for a brochure. tel. +44 (0)1908 858785; fax +44 (0)1908 858787; e-mail ouwenq@open.ac.uk

The Open University

Walton Hall, Milton Keynes

MK7 6AA

First published 2004

Edited, designed and typeset by The Open University.

Printed and bound in the United Kingdom by The Alden Group, Oxford.

ISBN 0 7492 5306 1

1.1

# Contents

# Course team

| | |
|---|---|
| Melanie Nind | *Joint chair and author* |
| Kieron Sheehy | *Joint chair and author* |
| Katy Simmons | *Author* |
| Jonathan Rix | *Author* |
| Mary Kellett | *Author* |
| Caroline Roaf | *Author* |
| Julie Allan | *External assessor* |
| Brenda Jarvis | *Course manager* |
| Liz Santucci | *Course secretary* |
| Alison Goslin | *Designer* |
| Sian Lewis | *Designer* |
| Isabel Ford | *Editor* |
| Fiona Carey | *Editor* |
| Chris Gravell | *Editor* |
| Nicola Tolcher | *Compositor* |
| Deana Plummer | *Picture researcher* |
| Demarisse Stanley | *Rights assistant* |
| Michael Peet | *BBC producer* |
| Ian Black | *BBC researcher* |
| Richard Fisher | *BBC Video editor* |
| Steve Hoy | *BBC Sound dubbing* |
| John Berry | *Critical reader* |
| John Swain | *Critical reader* |
| Sally French | *Critical reader* |
| Helen Murphy | *Critical reader* |
| Jim Towers | *Critical reader* |
| Ronnie Flynn | *Critical reader* |

# Introduction

In Book 3 we turn our attention to the need to listen to others so that we can learn from each other. We explore the perspectives on inclusive education held by academics, activists, learners, parents and professionals and what these mean for practice. We are also concerned with your own perspective, whether you are in any, some, or none of these roles.

The course has given you some tools for thinking about inclusive education: the models and discourses that we have covered in Books 1 and 2 give you a way of getting under the surface of what you see and read. We have not, however, given you any tidy definitions of what inclusive education actually is. This is because what we understand inclusive education to be depends very much on who we are, what our educational and other experiences have been and our own individual ideas about how education should be. In this sense, inclusive education is not a unified idea but a range of visions or concepts of inclusive education.

In Unit 5 you get to know one inner-city primary school which has worked hard to become more inclusive. You meet some of the staff, pupils and parents, and gain insights into how the different stakeholders in school think about what goes on there.

In Unit 6 and the following units you will see that there are some features that are common to a whole range of visions, definitions or concepts of inclusive education. Other aspects are more contested, however. We will not be telling you what is correct or incorrect, but we do ask you to read openly and critically and to make connections with your own ideas and experiences.

We begin with more theoretical perspectives in Unit 6 but move on to the perspectives of students and parents in Unit 7 and professionals in Unit 8. As Jenny Corbett argues:

> If we want to avoid atrophy in theorizing in inclusive education we need to be open to learn from those who experience it and those who do it. Disabled students and teachers should be part of the theorizing if they are to be fully supported in undertaking what is a challenging process of growth and collaborative development.
>
> *(Corbett, 2000, p. 171)*

## Reference

Corbett, J. (2000) 'Continuing the dialogue' in Clough, P. and Corbett, J. (eds) *Theories of Inclusive Education: a student's guide*, London, Paul Chapman.

# UNIT 5   Inclusion in progress

*Prepared for the course team by Jonathan Rix and Katy Simmons*

## Contents

# 1 Introduction

In this unit, and in the accompanying video, we look at inclusive practice at Bangabandhu School in the London Borough of Tower Hamlets through the perspectives and experiences of a range of adults who are connected with that school. First, though, we describe the context in which Bangabandhu operates. We look at the recent history of the funding of 'special educational needs' and at how the priorities of central government and local education authorities (LEAs) impact on inclusive practices.

While there is considerable local flexibility in policies and practices, the priorities of LEAs are based, to some extent, on the priorities set by national government. LEA performance, in England, is monitored by national bodies such as Ofsted and the Audit Commission. Details of funding and accountability may be different where you live: Ofsted, for example, has no remit in Scotland. But the example of Tower Hamlets LEA and the particular case study of Bangabandhu School allow us to see ways in which administrative structures can work to promote inclusion.

Bangabandhu School and the London Borough of Tower Hamlets were used as an example of good practice by the Audit Commission in its report *Special Educational Needs: a mainstream issue* (2002). In this unit we use this example to illustrate how national policies on inclusion can link dynamically with local policies in LEAs and with the aspirations of particular schools.

In Section 2 we set the context by outlining central government policy on inclusion, the statutory responsibilities of LEAs with regard to 'special educational needs' and the implications of the direct funding of schools. We then look at the particular circumstances of Tower Hamlets and the LEA's inclusive agenda.

In the remaining sections of the unit we use our observations, video footage and quotations from interviews with staff to conduct an in-depth exploration of practice at Bangabandhu School.

## Learning outcomes

By the end of this unit you will:

- have an understanding of how practices in school are influenced by many differing – often conflicting – discourses;
- understand how funding practices – based on history or on particular models of learning – influence how far particular LEAs and schools have moved towards inclusion;
- have an understanding of the complex factors that enable inclusive practice to be developed;

- understand that progress towards inclusive policies may depend on the history/geography/politics of where you live;
- be able to picture inclusive classrooms at work and be able to use your wider understandings from the course to evaluate what you see;
- have listened to the perspectives of one group of staff on how they understand and experience a particular school.

### Resources for this unit

For this unit you will need:

- Video Band A, part 1, 'A day in the journey of Bangabandhu'
- Chapter 7, 'Inclusion at Bangabandhu Primary School' by Cathy Phillips and Helen Jenner, in Reader 2.

## Activity 5.1   A journey in Tower Hamlets

Now read Chapter 7, 'Inclusion at Bangabandhu Primary School' by Cathy Phillips and Helen Jenner, in Reader 2. As you read, note all the different people, groups and organizations that have influenced the development of the school. We want you to bear these influences in mind as we set the school in its broader context.

The main influences we identified from Cathy Phillips and Helen Jenner's account were the impact of pupils, parents and policy makers at both local and national level, as well as the wider social setting of the school. Bangabandhu is both shaping its own destiny and being shaped by outside forces.

## 2   Local education authorities and 'special educational needs'

The 1981 Education Act gave LEAs statutory responsibilities for identifying and assessing children who 'have or may possibly have' special educational needs, for the writing and maintaining of statements of special educational need and for the arrangement of provision detailed on those statements. But each LEA was left to devise its own methods of supporting pupils who have such needs. As a result, services and provision developed unevenly in different LEAs, and LEAs continue to vary enormously in terms of numbers of pupils with statements/records of need, the use of segregated provision and the development of more integrated and inclusive provision. It matters where you live, as Figure 5.1 shows.

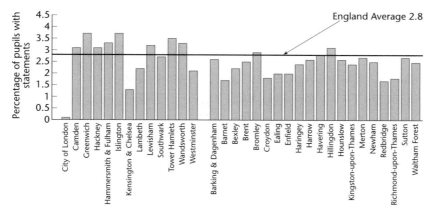

*Figure 5.1    Variation in percentages of pupils with statements of special educational needs in different London LEA areas, January 1997(DfEE, 1997, p. 39).*

These variations in provision have persisted, even as LEAs' powers have declined. The 1988 Education Act introduced local management of schools (LMS) and required that the majority of LEAs' education budgets be passed directly to schools. Peter Gray (2002) pointed out that 'this was intended to allow headteachers and governors greater discretion to decide what external services they needed, if any, to meet the educational needs of their pupils' (p. 5). It was the Government's view that the quality and efficiency of education would improve if decisions about how money was spent were made at school level rather than by LEAs.

The 1999 Fair Funding initiative put even more pressure on LEAs to delegate increasing proportions of the schools' budget to schools themselves, as 'frontline providers of high standards in the classroom' (DfEE, 2000, p. 3). Spending on special educational needs, which had previously been ring-fenced as an LEA responsibility, could, under Fair Funding, be delegated to schools.

Despite the increase in direct funding to schools, central government still attempts to exert influence on policy and practice at LEA level. The Schools Forum, established in each LEA in January 2003, exists to advise the LEA on its spending in the light of local interests, but, as Peter Downes comments, 'The government is keen to see local formulae reflecting the national priorities' (2003, p. 2).

That said, although all schools and LEAs in England work within a framework established in law, that framework is enabling rather than prescriptive. This means that local interpretation of national legislation can vary considerably. Brian Goacher and his colleagues have described the relationship between central government and LEAs as 'a delicately balanced partnership', with 'good will' essential from all parties (Goacher *et al.*, 1988, p. 2).

We can see this delicate balance in action in the guidance offered by central government to LEAs on how resources can be distributed to support inclusion. The opening paragraphs of the guidance acknowledge the interrelationship of central and local government and the reluctance of central government to dictate local practice:

> The development of inclusion and raising attainment for all pupils are key Government priorities ...
>
> The Government does not intend to impose common funding arrangements, as it is clear that local discussion and agreement are critical to the development of effective practice ...
>
> *(DfES, 2002, paras 1.1.1, 1.1.2)*

Schools receive a considerable amount of funding through a process of decision making at local level and not all decision-makers share a commitment to inclusion. As Carol Vincent *et al.* (1996) pointed out, some decision-makers who superficially use the language of inclusion are actually holding on to deficit-based, medical models of learning difficulty.

In contrast, commitment to inclusion at LEA level can lead to major changes within individual schools. We will see this process in action in Chapter 10 in Reader 2, where Carol Bannister *et al.* describe the way that a special school for pupils with physical disabilities became an inclusion service, providing a range of support for children attending local mainstream schools. Though the school was run by the charity Barnardo's, the involvement of Somerset, the local LEA, was a crucial part of the total project, particularly in its early stages.

## LEAs and inclusion

In 2000 a government policy document on the role of LEAs redefined their 'precise and limited functions' as follows:

- special educational needs

- access – school transport and admission arrangements, school attendance

- school improvement – responsibility for schools in serious weaknesses or special measures/excluded children/behaviour support plans

- strategic management – develop policy, set priorities, allocate resources

> *(DfEE, 2000, p. 3)*

Despite being pushed further to the margins by national policy changes, LEAs are still, then, major players in provision for pupils with additional needs.

Three years earlier, in 1997, the incoming New Labour government had published its Green Paper, *Excellence for All Children* (DfEE, 1997). The Green Paper not only declared, 'We want to see more pupils with SEN included within mainstream primary and secondary schools' (DfEE, 1997, p. 44), but also recorded the government's support for the UNESCO Salamanca Statement of 1994.

A study conducted by Alan Dyson and his colleagues between April 1999 and March 2000 reflects what Felicity Fletcher-Campbell (2002) has called the 'implementation gap', that is, the gap between government intention and local practice. Asked about their views on the special educational needs Code of Practice, their funding of additional provision in mainstream schools and their 'philosophy', some LEAs reported a commitment to developing greater inclusion. (As is common practice in such study reports, the LEAs are given fictitious names.)

> Some respondents spoke of a 'strong move' in this direction (Forestshire), or of being 'very positive' with a 'strong commitment' (Carville). For others, however, the commitment was qualified by reference to 'the normal constraints that apply' (Borderland), or the need for 'a gentle reorganisation' (Riverborough), or a 'pragmatic' approach (Fernshire).
>
> *(Dyson* et al., *2002, p. 19)*

Dyson's study shows that it was not just the level of commitment to inclusion that varied. Each LEA experienced different barriers to inclusion: 'Borderland' had had serious budget problems, 'Chalkshire' was struggling with rising numbers of statements and 'Carville', recently reorganized as a unitary authority, was still formalizing its policies. Not only did the LEAs experience great variability, but they also felt the impact of different constraints as they moved, at different speeds, towards more inclusive practice.

The mechanisms that LEAs use to distribute their resources can also have a major impact on the development of inclusive practices. Felicity Fletcher-Campbell (2002) examined the way in which systems can help or hinder the development of successful inclusion. She identifies three basic models, each of which represents political decisions, taken in the context of scarce or limited resources. In summary, these models are:

- Direct funding of special schools.

  This model led to dissatisfaction among those wanting inclusion and led to a greater proportion of the available budget going on non-educational matters such as diagnosis and litigation.

- Decentralization of decision making to the most local level possible.

  This model created general satisfaction and fewer negative unintended outcomes. Practitioners were more directly involved.

- Budgets attached to particular pupils.

  This model created difficulties, as parents tended to vie for the highest amounts possible. Schools, in turn, welcomed those pupils with the highest budgets attached to them, but involving the minimum of additional work.

Fletcher-Campbell concludes that:

> Overall, the study suggests that inclusion is best served by decentralized systems of resourcing – which shorten lines of communication, are responsive to local need and preferences and nearest to the pupil ... Systems which encourage schools to collaborate, rather than compete, with each other favour inclusion.
>
> *(Fletcher-Campbell, 2002, p. 21)*

Her conclusions about funding mechanisms are, however, tentative and she comments that resourcing policies are 'not everything' (p. 22).

##  Activity 5.2    Local forces

Jot down in your learning journal some of the pressures within an LEA that might lead to changes towards more inclusive provision in schools.

The pressures we noted include the following:

- central government policies
- financial incentives
- pressure from local parents and young people
- pressure from local groups of disabled adults
- political views of elected members.

On reflection, though, it seemed to us that all of these pressures could equally well be applied by those who want to keep segregated and non-inclusive provision in place. It is not surprising, then, that movement towards inclusion has often been a battleground, politically fraught and hotly contested. It has taken deeply-held conviction, aligned with political power, to bring about inclusive practices in many LEAs. Perhaps the best-known example of an LEA that has based its developing policies on principle is the London Borough of Newham.

*Figure 5.2*   Map of London – the location of the London Boroughs of Newham and Tower Hamlets

The London Borough of Newham shares a border with Tower Hamlets, the focus of this unit. The two boroughs have much in common, with very diverse minority ethnic populations and significant areas of unemployment and social deprivation. Inclusion has, however, been accepted in Newham as a cornerstone of LEA policy since 1986. Newham's story shows that there are many factors in the journey towards inclusive local provision. These factors can include determined parents, the involvement of disabled adults and sustained political activity. Alongside these factors, the history and commitment of the LEA can have a defining impact, and the LEA can take a leadership role, either in promoting or in holding back inclusive practice. Tower Hamlet's move towards inclusion was more recent.

## Tower Hamlets

The London Borough of Tower Hamlets serves what Ofsted, in its September 1998 report, described as 'a largely disadvantaged population', where unemployment was high, where more than double the national average of pupils were entitled to free school meals and where 'poverty, poor housing and indifferent health are the reality for many inhabitants of the Borough' (Ofsted, 1998, para. 6). Despite the large amounts of money spent on education in Tower Hamlets, Ofsted described educational achievement in the Borough as 'unacceptably low at all levels' (Ofsted, 1998, para. 8). Provision for 'special educational needs' was described as 'variable in effectiveness':

There is rapid and unchecked growth in statements in the
secondary phase, no clear strategy based on analysis of
needs and no evaluation of the effectiveness of provision.

*(Ofsted, 1998, para. 15)*

Overall, Ofsted described the LEA as 'facing massive and necessary
change' (1998, para. 5) and made a number of recommendations as
to what those changes should be, prior to further inspection.

By the time the LEA was re-inspected in June 2000, much of that
change had been set in motion. The new policy, 'Towards inclusive
education in schools: policy and strategy', agreed in January 1999,
was a major part of the LEA's improvement agenda. A new post of
head of inclusive education was created, along with an inclusive
education steering group, comprising LEA officers, headteachers and
representatives of parents and other agencies. The changes were
focused on 'raising standards for all pupils through making the best
use of the funding available' (Ofsted, 2000, p. 52). Ofsted reported a
'significant attitudinal change' in many schools, which had come to
accept that they, not the LEA, should accept responsibility for pupils
(Ofsted, 2000, para. 53).

Helen Jenner, who took on the role of leading the LEA's inclusion
policy initiative, described it to us as 'fundamental to attainment and
improving the quality of teaching and learning and the culture and
ethos of all of our schools'. As part of her job, Helen works directly
with service providers such as the education social work service or
health service, looking at ways of improving access to education. She
also has a role in informing elected members of the council of the
views of the local community, using newly-created local area
partnerships to feed into the council's decision-making process. The
process of seeking views is an active one:

> We've also learned that actually if you want people to
> come to meetings, it's no good saying 'come to a meeting
> about Tower Hamlets inclusive education policy' – that
> doesn't mean anything to anyone. You need to go out to
> people ... there's some good examples of the sort of
> consultation that we do around Sure Start where we train
> up local people to go and talk one-to-one to local people
> in shops, in cafes, in restaurants, to try and get a broad
> picture

*(E243 Video, Band A, video pages 129–30)*

Helen Jenner describes the 'cultural shift' in Tower Hamlets that has
made it possible to find out from local people what they want and
what they think about education. She describes the LEA as 'a learning
education authority':

What I think happens in Tower Hamlets is that for teachers, the challenge of working here means that you have a really diverse population to work with ... you don't feel like you're the expert so you're happy to go and learn. You never get it right in Tower Hamlets and nobody expects you to: everybody expects you to be striving ... people are very happy then to explore and approach new ideas. I think what we try to do is give people the confidence to take some risks ... Start from where they are and move on to the next challenge and support people in moving forward.

*(Helen Jenner, E243 Video, Band A, video pages 136–7, 139, 141)*

Helen Jenner sees learning as a fundamental part of the LEA's inclusive agenda:

People have to know that sometimes that will work, but actually if it doesn't you'll have learned anyway ... That's the message we give to children too. That's how they learn. I think that's how we learn as adults.

*(Helen Jenner, E243 Video, Band A, video page 142)*

This agenda is reflected in Bangabandhu School's Inclusion Policy:

We recognize that by adopting an inclusive education approach we have had to enter a process that involves changing and challenging systems and structures and adapting the curriculum; the buildings; the language, images and role models.

*(Bangabandhu Inclusion Policy)*

Linda Chesworth, acting head, confirmed that the school policy is part of school life: 'We take inclusion very seriously, we're ... passionate about that and basically we think it's every child's right to have access to a full curriculum.'

Inclusion in Tower Hamlets became part of an overall strategy of school improvement after Ofsted's highly critical inspection of the LEA in 1998. By 2000, when Ofsted revisited, the policy was deemed successful not just because of its positive educational outcomes but also because it had helped curtail the LEA's spiralling expenditure on special educational needs and expensive out-of-borough placements. The development of LEA policy nurtured the development of schools such as Bangabandhu, underlining their commitment to diversity and access.

## 3 A staff-eye view: inclusion at Bangabandhu School

### Background

In this section we consider inclusive practice in the context of Bangabandhu School in Tower Hamlets, exploring the beliefs of some of the staff and examining examples of their practice in action. We spoke to the deputy headteacher, the special needs co-ordinator (SENCO), 4 other teachers from a teaching staff of 27 and 4 teaching assistants (TAs) from a TA staff of 25. Two of the TAs were also midday supervisors and one was a member of the cleaning staff. We acknowledge that this represents a limited perspective and that our research would have been even more valuable had we included the views of pupils and parents.

Despite our limited sample group, we feel the values expressed are widely shared in the school and that this is an essential factor in the school's progress towards inclusive practice across the whole school. We do not suggest that we are describing a perfect inclusive school, nor that we have discovered a school that has 'achieved' inclusion. We see inclusive practice as an ongoing process – a moment-to-moment attempt to respond positively to those involved in the community of a school. Inevitably, within those moments, all those involved are being physically, socially and cognitively included and excluded to varying degrees (Blamires, 1999). Bangabandhu is, however, a school that makes clear its belief in inclusion and that has made a series of decisions based on this belief. It is therefore worth examining its practices to see how it attempts to promote inclusion for all. In carrying out this examination we can find out a great deal about the kind of inclusive education that is worth aspiring to.

We would not pretend that Bangabandhu is all schools to all people. Like every school, Bangabandhu exists in a particular social and cultural context. In many ways it includes a wider diversity of pupil than many schools simply because of where it is. It would be naive to dismiss the relevance of its experiences to other situations because of this, however. Every school draws upon a wide variety of cultures and social experiences; after all, no two homes are ever quite the same. The obviousness of differences at Bangabandhu makes it easier to identify and examine broad adaptations to the school system, but when considering how the school has responded to those differences we must remember that inclusion is not about meeting the needs of particular groups. It is about working with individual pupils and all that they bring to the learning situation. In this way Bangabandhu is no different to any school.

Similarly, much that we describe in this unit is not radically different from good practice developed and used by many schools and teachers over the years. What seems to be fundamentally different is the genuine attempt to apply it to all pupils within the local community and the commitment of all to achieving the inclusive goals.

## Statements of principle

### An inclusive agenda

The Bangabandhu School prospectus states:

> We are committed to offering a place to any child in the neighbourhood. We aim to provide high-quality learning opportunities for **all** children whatever their needs. We have a purpose built school and welcome children with disabilities. Significant additional facilities will be added to the school in 2002/3 to enable us to provide for a wider range of special educational need.
>
> *(Bangabandhu Prospectus 2001–2002, p. 13)*

Since the school has established an inclusive agenda for itself, it seems sensible for us to consider what is meant by 'inclusion' for the school and those working within it. The school has set out its beliefs in an Inclusion Policy, which has a set of principles, aims, definitions and objectives.

### The Inclusion Policy

> We consider all the children in the immediate neighbourhood have a right to attend our school. Every child has the same right of access and is entitled to

appropriate support to meet their individual needs. Children with physical, learning *or* sensory disabilities or emotional or behavioural difficulties have a right to the support they need in our classrooms. Our school community is open, positive and diverse and our school is accessible to staff, parents and carers with disabilities. We believe developing an inclusive approach to all aspects of school life can act as a pathway towards inclusion in the wider community.

*(Bangabandhu Inclusion Policy)*

The policy goes on to set out the right of children to learn and play together. It states that it is discrimination to exclude someone as a consequence of their disability, and it explains the advantages to the pupils and the school of inclusive practices. It also outlines the need for flexibility and adaptability on behalf of all individuals and systems involved with the school.

We recognise that by adopting an inclusive education approach we have had to enter a process that involves changing and challenging systems and structures and adapting the curriculum; the buildings; the language, images and role-models. We also recognise that inclusion is not a single issue but involves a wide range of options and depends on a range of factors that include the individual, the setting and available resources.

*(Bangabandhu Inclusion Policy)*

These principles were reflected, too, in comments made by staff.

I just think you've just got to do the best ... it's my job and my duty to do the best that I can for that child. (Sarah, class teacher)

We found that it's been very difficult to make a general rule if you like of how the children should be treated, whether they should be taught in class or out of class, but we've come to the conclusion that every child's an individual and we have to make a programme to suit the individual needs of that child. (SENCO)

Bangabandhu, then, has clear statements of principle, but we need to be able to focus more precisely on the processes that result from these generalized principles.

## From principle to process

### Researching inclusion

Lindsay and Dockrell (2002) point out that inclusion is difficult to research as a whole and needs to be broken down into 'specific variables'. Breaking down inclusive practice into individual bullet points risks creating the educational version of a medical model, though. When we separate and define each component we imply that they are independent of each other and can function in isolation. This is clearly not the case. When inclusive education occurs consistently and not just as isolated moments these factors will be seen to operate as part of an overlapping and intertwined whole. To help you explore that whole and your place within it, however, we *are* using bullet points to focus discussion. Whether this is inclusive practice will depend on your response.

We have created our bullet points through an analysis of interviews with Bangabandhu staff and general discussions regarding the video footage recorded in the school. You will examine the list in the next activity. The terms that we have come up with are not those used by people at the school, nor are they derived from any specific model of inclusion, but they are intended to draw together strands and themes within the interviews and discussions. It is important to remind you that because we are focusing on the staff's perspective we have not involved pupils' wishes, aims or goals and interests, and that this should be an important part of any inclusive setting.

## An inclusive school culture

The overriding premise at Bangabandhu seems to be for inclusive practice to be founded upon diverse cultures and experiences reflected in all aspects of the curriculum. Our use of the term 'curriculum' is very broad. It includes ideas of the formal and informal curriculum, the observable and hidden, the intended and the actual. There are formal activities for which the school allocates particular time and resources, and informal activities that occur outside this timetable or outside the school or school day. There are stated and observable policies and practices, and hidden meanings and signals. There are the intended outcomes of the systems and the structures, and there are the actual consequences of the day-to-day experience of being within them. 'Curriculum', therefore, includes educational matters, such as what is taught in the class, how it is taught, who teaches it and who is being taught, and also pastoral, social and administrative activities.

If diversity is reflected in all aspects of the curriculum it should encourage a supportive learning culture. We use the term 'culture' as defined by Schein (1984). For Schein, a culture operates at different levels, in its visible artefacts, values and basic underlying assumptions. The visible artefacts include the built environment, available technology, dress code, communication patterns and public documentation. The values are the negotiable reasons that are given for what is being done and why it is being done. Underlying assumptions are the beliefs that underpin thinking, that are taken for granted and are difficult to question or to change. The three levels of culture interconnect, affecting and being affected by each other. Unpicking this interconnective structure can reveal many chicken and egg issues, but responses to these issues will of themselves reveal much about the culture.

A supportive culture will have artefacts, values and assumptions that are in tune with each other. There will be few contradictions between what is seen, what is stated and what is fundamentally believed. For it to be supportive of learning, the culture will need to reveal artefacts, values and assumptions that all attempt to maximize the physical, social and cognitive development of all pupils. For example, in the video you will hear a teacher describe how problems in the playground have been resolved by discussion with pupils and the purchase of new play equipment.

## A bullet list for inclusion?

On the basis of the comments of staff at Bangabandhu, we identified four cornerstones of the school culture: the breaking down of disabling barriers; open communication; individual and group self-control; and full access and participation for all.

The breaking down of disabling barriers is pro-active. It is about identifying those aspects of school life that restrict access, communication or self-control. Open communication is about the effective and unrestricted movement of people and ideas. Individual and group self-control is concerned with the ownership of issues and ways of operating, and responsibility towards and respect for others' rights. Full access and participation for all reflects the school principles, but offers a means of measuring the success of the other cultural cornerstones.

The Bangabandhu staff assert, in different ways, that to achieve this inclusive learning culture requires the following:

- positive role models
- secure and valued pupils
- varied teaching approaches
- varied tasks, materials, equipment and groupings
- challenging and appropriate learning tasks
- focus and motivation through relevance of tasks
- clear, relevant, assessment and feedback.

Always bearing in mind that the aspects listed here are not discrete but are part of an integrated whole, we can further break down the inclusive practice identified at Bangabandhu as being founded upon:

◆ diverse cultures and experiences reflected in all aspects of the curriculum
  *encouraging:*
  - a supportive learning culture
    *built upon:*
    → the breaking down of disabling barriers
    → open communication
    → individual and group self-control
    → full participation and access for all
      *requiring:*
      ⇒ positive role models
      ⇒ secure pupils
      ⇒ valued pupils
      ⇒ active listening and communication with pupils
      ⇒ varied teaching approaches
      ⇒ varied materials
      ⇒ varied tasks
      ⇒ varied grouping
      ⇒ varied equipment
      ⇒ challenging learning tasks
      ⇒ appropriate learning tasks
      ⇒ focus through relevance
      ⇒ motivation through relevance
      ⇒ assessment in context of experience
      ⇒ clear feedback

▷ # Activity 5.3   Aiming high

In the box below is a list of Bangabandhu's aims. Read the aims and compare them with our list above. To what degree and in what ways do you feel that our list, based on the staff's descriptions, coincides with the school's stated aims? Which of the school's stated aims do you think will specifically enhance inclusion? Can you begin to prioritize these aims in order of their impact on inclusive practice?

This exercise will help you to rehearse thinking skills needed for TMA 03.

---

**Aims**

The staff, governors, children and parents of Bangabandhu are aiming to establish the school as one of the highest quality. We define this as one that:

- has clear, stated aims and goals
- acts as a community
- offers a broad and balanced curriculum where the individual needs of the children are taken into account

- seeks to help each child reach their potential in all areas
- inspires confidence
- has a strong positive ethos of caring and fostering responsibility and respect for others
- values cultural differences and diversity
- recognises contributions of all individuals
- values the child/parent/teacher partnership
- provides a safe, secure environment
- plans for the future and makes progressive changes
- provides attractive, well-organised and resourced working areas
- has a good relationship with the neighbourhood and the local community and seeks to build links with outside agencies
- continues to attract and retain good quality staff
- continues to attract pupils
- continually compares itself with other schools to ensure standards of achievement constantly rise

(*Bangabandhu Prospectus*)

You may have found considerable overlap between the school's aims and our bullet list. For example, there may be links between the aim of the 'ethos of caring' and the 'secure and valued pupils', or you may have connected 'values the child/parent/teacher partnership' with 'full participation and access for all'. You may feel that to 'help each child reach their potential in all areas' will require all of the bullet points to be operative; if they are not, there may be a risk of help being misdirected, creating personal, social or educational problems for a child.

You might also feel that much of the list deals with the sorts of good practice that all schools aspire to. Equally, when prioritizing the aims in relation to inclusion you may have been able to establish a clear order. This list may reflect your own relationship with education, of course. For example, if you are a learning support assistant reading this you may feel that 'recognises contributions of all individuals' is more significant than 'compares itself with other schools', whereas if you are from an LEA you may reverse the priority. You may initially have felt that some aims were clearly more important than others, but after consideration begin to see considerable overlaps in significance. One thing is guaranteed, if you discuss this list with others you will have to consider your priorities again.

## Diverse in name, diverse in nature?

So what examples are there of diverse cultures and experiences being reflected in all aspects of the curriculum? Clearly, the formal, published prospectus and policies express the school's intention to reflect diversity within the curriculum; the serving of Halal meat and vegetarian dishes demonstrates it in action. So, too, does the choice of a school name that honours a founder of Bangladesh and the decoration of the school hall with hangings produced by local community projects. The weekly Olympic Club, with facilities specifically focused on people disabled by typical playground activities, reflects a commitment to all too, as does the encouragement given to individuals to use the languages spoken at home in a variety of situations. In many formal and informal ways, we can see that positive signals are given out that support the principle.

This does not mean, however, that the diversity of cultures and experiences are always being reflected. Much of the school is decorated with standard, mainstream academic posters and materials specifically linked to learning targets. Much of what is taught in the classroom is inevitably defined by the national curriculum and this limits, to a certain degree, the flexibility in reflecting diverse cultures and experiences within lesson time. Nonetheless, staff mentioned their practice of relating prescribed topics to personal experience, and the importance of using multicultural and bilingual texts:

> I think you've got to have a variety of activities that are just interesting for all the children. In terms of, for example, literacy, our stories have to be ... sometimes we have sort of ... we have multicultural stories. It's not just focusing on text which are solely for children who are English-speaking for example. We encourage a variety of text. (Sarah, class teacher)

This tension between the national standards and local community experience is bound to underlie the vast majority of day-to-day activity within the school, however. It is a tension that you may have noted when contrasting the list of inclusive practice on page 25 with the stated aims of Bangabandhu in Activity 5.3.

> I think it's nice to have that time in the morning just to sit and listen because it's always not just about 'they have to learn and they've got to know about 1+1 = 2': it's all about sharing, it's all about social interaction and appreciating each other. (Sarah, class teacher)

# 4  A supportive learning culture?

On entering Bangabandhu it is not immediately obvious to an able-bodied person what unusual school buildings they are. It seems to be like most schools. It is only when you notice the width of corridors, the absence of steps, doors and raised doorways that you begin to appreciate the accessible built environment. The school buildings are, however, only one of the visible artefacts. Within every classroom there is evidence of equipment that reflects the learning needs of pupils and staff.

As Katie, a class teacher explained:

> the school is really well resourced, so normally if you haven't got it in classroom, somebody else will have what you need or it will be in one of the stock cupboards, so we don't have to get into that 'have we got enough money for things', we can normally ask, and it's provided. It never, never feels like a huge issue.

## ○ Activity 5.4   A day in the journey of Bangabandhu

Watch Video Band A, part 1, 'A day in the journey of Bangabandhu', up to the point where the children finish singing and leave the hall (video page 18). When you have finished viewing, use a table like the one below to list visible artefacts within the school that demonstrate principles of inclusion or which work against these principles.

| VISIBLE ARTEFACTS | | | | | |
|---|---|---|---|---|---|
| Built environment | Available technology | Dress code | Communication patterns | Public documentation | Other |
| | | | | | |

After making your list, you may find it useful to watch the video again and/or talk about the visible artefacts with someone else who has seen the video and then revise your list. You will probably have noticed some different things.

You probably noted the wide corridors and open hallway at Bangabandhu. You may have noticed the different cultural clothing, the sense of belonging different people express, and the open communication. You may have considered the manner in which displays reflect the local community and demonstrate pride in pupils and their work. All of these can be regarded as visible evidence of a supportive learning culture. In this clip we did not see any evidence of artefacts working against inclusive principles.

Underpinning the visible artefacts are the stated values. We considered a number of the formally stated values in Section 3, but they also came through during discussions with staff:

> The school tries to address things. It provides for our kind of either renewed education or initial training, addressing those issues so they are part of the school consciousness. (Andrew, support teacher)

> What is important to me, is that he's interacting with his peers, he's enjoying being at school and he's just really enjoying what he does. (Sarah, class teacher)

> I think one of the problems with the statementing process at the moment is that child has to fail before the resources are available whereas we try and jump in before we get to that stage, if the needs are that bad. (SENCO)

In all of these quotes we can feel the whisper of Bangabandhu's written aims. These comments could well be just the espoused values of the school. We need to see whether the values are truly reflected in the underlying assumptions. For example, the SENCO underlines the tension between formal procedure and the need to respond speedily to an individual's learning needs. This demonstrates the principle contained within the school's Inclusion Policy that 'we have had to enter a process that involves changing and challenging systems'.

However, at the end of her sentence she uses the phrase 'if the needs are that bad'. This phrase raises a number of questions about underlying assumptions and therefore about the validity of the espoused values. Can a pupil's learning needs be 'bad'? Who are they bad for? What are 'good' needs? Other questions are raised too. Will staff 'jump in' only for pupils who are failing? And how do they measure failure? Is this in relation to a fixed notional standard, or based on an assessment of a pupil in the context of their expectations and experiences?

Of course, analysing one spoken statement in a written form in this much detail without setting it in context and comparing it with other statements is likely to produce an inaccurate reading. It is difficult to make hard and fast judgements about other people's beliefs. If we wish to feel that we are approaching an accurate analysis of underlying assumptions, we need to find actions or patterns of behaviour that support value statements.

## Bringing down barriers?

At Bangabandhu, staff comments offered us evidence of their underlying assumption that their role is to break down disabling barriers, to operate in open communication, to encourage individual and group self-control, and to strive for full participation and access for all.

So what evidence is there for the first of these, the breaking down of disabling barriers?

 ## Activity 5.5   Removing barriers

In the comments quoted below staff demonstrated a concern with removing barriers to cognitive, physical and social inclusion. As you read the quotes consider what barriers are being removed and how effective the methods are in removing them. Consider, too, what the wider impact may be on other pupils. In what way could we see the removal of barriers as positive actions increasing accessibility?.

---

The way I've modified my whole class is inclusive for Shahel because he can get around. The way it was chopped up before there were lots of tables. I've taken loads of tables out and made it more open space and open planned so he can get around. (Sarah, class teacher)

Acknowledgement, congratulations, erm, praise, erm ... it's about drawing children out who don't often, often make comments. (Andrew, support teacher)

PECS is a picture exchange communication – this is what really help him in his vocabulary. I mean this is what really help him in his speech because when he started in the school, he doesn't talk at all, he doesn't talk to anybody, he's withdrawing. But now, with that PECS, when this, when the school send me for the training, and um when I started with him, I show him whatever him wants, he has to give me the picture of what he wants, and then I will in turn I mean assist him or support him. (Felix, learning support assistant)

We invested a lot of time into learning styles about a year or two ... ago. It started off at quite a senior level and then we had a whole day and we've come back to it in a number of whole-day things and I think that's filtering through to kind of subconscious practice a lot. (Andrew, support teacher)

I think it helps having um one staff room actually, I think that, even though we are squashed in there, it ensures everybody is a part of that, and we've changed the seating lots of times. I think little things like that really make a difference. (Member of the senior management team)

We saw barriers taking a range of forms. Sometimes they require a major physical change. As a consequence of Sarah's reorganization of the tables, for example, all pupils had a greater freedom within their own classroom, which could well impact on their view of learning.

The removal of other barriers may require an attitudinal shift. For example, there has been change in people's attitudes to learning styles as a result of training sessions.

Removing barriers can mean a one-off change or it can be ongoing; the barriers may be small or they may be major.

## Open communication?

When you come to watch the rest of the video band in the next activity you will see a number of examples of open communication between staff, between pupils, and between staff and pupils. Perhaps the clearest symbol of this openness is the use of first names by everyone involved in the school, reducing a sense of 'them and us' and making it easier for people to approach one another both formally and informally.

> When I started teaching ... it felt really odd with the children I teach calling me Vanessa and I thought they weren't going to respect me, but it's not an issue at all. It really isn't. (Vanessa, class teacher)

There seems to be a genuine attempt to maintain open communication between all levels of the school organization. Typically, support staff are included in training days and staff meetings. Their presence was also considered to be essential by management when organizing a school conference on the development of inclusion.

Many of the teaching approaches encourage openness too. There is clearly a dividing line whereby the class teacher is the ultimate arbiter of what occurs in the lesson, but, nonetheless, all the staff we spoke to highlighted their ability to discuss classroom practice and lesson organization in an open and frank manner.

> But we always, in passing even, sort of: 'Great, that did work. They have got that.' Or: 'We might have to work on that again because it's not.' (Janis, learning support assistant)

This openness can also be seen in the assessment of pupils and the evaluation of their learning.

> During each lesson I normally try to write some comments in the class books, their maths books or English books. And then at the end of the lesson I do speak to the class teacher and let her know whether the lesson went well or whether I needed to adapt it to suit the child I was working with. (Janis, learning support assistant)

We also came across occasions when a pupil's evaluation of their own learning needs was taken into consideration. In the following example, a visually-impaired pupil was able to improve the production of her own learning materials by highlighting the difficulty she had in understanding mathematical problems when they were laid out horizontally across the page.

> We did a lot of work through the maths system, which is very interesting, where we did all the preparation and gave her the paper which was in a format which we thought would work for her and then she came back to us afterwards. That was quite a learning experience because there were a lot of things that we hadn't quite seen as being visual issues which she was struggling with. (Andrew, support teacher)

For some pupils the commitment to encouraging them to communicate their feelings and requirements openly is built into their daily routine. The following example refers to a boy who has been defined as autistic.

> Another important thing that happen is they have choice. If they come in in the morning, it depend on what the mood is, if it's not very good at all we ask him what is he going to do, and if he feels so tired, then we give him the choice – tell us exactly what you want to do. (Felix, learning support assistant)

## Who's in charge of your learning?

In a school in which individual pupil need is given priority and in which communications are open, there is a clear requirement for all members of the school community to be aware of their responsibilities to others around them and to take them seriously. For this to occur effectively, those in a position of authority will have to model appropriate behaviour.

A number of examples in classes we observed demonstrated a willingness to place trust in pupils. They were able to leave of their own volition if they needed to use the toilet, but they were expected to sign a book on leaving. Generally, it was noted that the system was not misused, though one pupil did leave the room twice in one lesson having not left during the previous lesson when her interest seemed somewhat greater. We were also told, for example, about a boy who was teased because he was reading simple texts, and how the teacher combatted this by making some of the most able readers responsible for listening to and assisting the boy with his reading, while he became responsible for listening and commenting on their reading. (We cannot say whether this particular pupil liked peer support in this form.)

> It's all part of inclusion for me: just not having things so teacher-led or adult-led; they need to be able to just go ahead and feel secure and safe and just do things on their own. (Sarah, class teacher)

This sense of shared responsibility was also clearly evident in the interactions between staff. Though some support staff did tend to work with just one or two of the pupils, they all expressed their belief that they could guide their own teaching.

> In terms of shifts of powers, as far as the children are concerned we're all adults, we're all teachers. There's not: 'OK, Sarah's the teacher and this person does this and that person ... ' you know. I have a great respect for everybody. We are the teachers, the adults within my class and it's not just: 'I'm a teacher and you're this and you're that so you have to listen to me.' That's just not the way I work. So in terms of with Ruby, if she wants to modify things, which she does all the time, feel free go ahead with it. It's all for the better of the children ... (Sarah, class teacher)

There were a number of instances, too, in which it was evident that the pupils were leading their own learning, or in which pupils were allowed to define how their learning was delivered.

> But when they were singing it was just, I don't know, it was just them being more in control, them sort of

teaching me things. I think that's what it's all about really. (Sarah, class teacher)

She doesn't like feeling as if she's got to have lots and lots of extra support and it being made obvious. So I will just chat really quietly with her, you know: is she OK with this, does she need any enlarging, or does she need to sit nearer say when we're watching a video or something. But I wouldn't kind of do it in a loud way because she doesn't like that. (Katie, class teacher)

It was also commonplace for pupils to be given time to think and discuss, and be allowed to evaluate and express their own perspectives on an issue.

I don't get them paired up. Normally it's just turn to the person next to you, if you need to. So some of them just prefer to work independently and others do have to discuss if they're finding things difficult. They kind of know before they come to me, they can speak quietly to someone on their table, to try and get them to help them or tell them where things are going wrong. (Vanessa, class teacher)

In a couple of cases pupils were given considerable control over matters of social significance. For example, the school operates a 'circle of friends' for pupils who feel excluded at break times. This is a support group of peers who volunteer to play with the one who feels isolated. There was also discussion of empowering pupils to sort out their own personal and group differences.

It would be inappropriate, however, to suggest that pupils have considerable amounts of power handed to them. For example, when a group was brought together to solve the playground problems it was not selected by pupils but by teaching staff, who identified those pupils who they believed to be having the greatest difficulties.

One of the most interesting developments in group self-control is the growing self-belief within the school that staff have the ability and knowledge to satisfy the needs of their pupils without always calling on outside agencies. This growing self-confidence is a tribute to their inclusive practice that promises much for the future.

So I think all the staff, teaching assistants and teachers, are getting very, well, building up their expertise in all the different needs the children have … I mean there's so much expertise within the school … we're looking … well, within, much more than when we started. (SENCO)

## One in, all in?

There is evidence of full participation and access for pupils, staff and parents at Bangabandhu. The nature of the built environment is inclusive for the vast majority of people who would wish to come to the school. The operation of clubs such as the Olympic Club, which you will see on the video, offers opportunities for some involvement of all pupils in out-of-class activities. The school cleaners are included in weekend conferences on inclusion. The annual international evening and the summertime Mela (fête) both offer opportunities for parents and families to mix and experience diverse foods and cultures. Parents are invited regularly into assembly too, as well as to the more traditional parents' evenings.

The drive for parental participation and access is backed up by a commitment to the use of the languages of the home. There is a large number of bilingual staff who work closely with both parents and pupils.

> Most of the parents don't speak English, so obviously when something's happened in school, we need to relay it back to the parents and they'll, you'll probably see they come to us, and if something's lost, because they can't obviously speak to the teacher, because they can't make themselves understood. And parent interviews, we're there translating as well. (Ruby, teaching assistant)

Such a commitment clearly has social and academic consequences. For example, parents who are not literate in English sometimes express concern that they cannot help their children with their reading.

> We've told them it's important that they actually read with their children, it doesn't matter what language it's in so, um, they weren't aware of there being dual languages book until we pointed it out and it seems to have worked with them now. (Ruby, teaching assistant)

Another example of this parental involvement came through discussion with one parent about how the school had handled the 'diagnosis' of his son's autism. The parent made much of the support he had received and the discussions in which he had been involved. Most important of all to the parent, however, was that his son had become just another member of the class.

The school will always be measured by what actually happens in the classroom, of course. As you will see on the video, there are many comments that demonstrate the staff's belief that they work effectively, involving everyone in close-knit teams. There are some suggestions by teachers, however, that support staff will often work with a prescribed group of pupils only, reducing their participation and isolating those pupils. We saw some evidence of this, but it was equally evident that some members of staff were aware of the shortcomings of this approach and attempted to rectify them.

> It's really easy for the teaching assistant to only work with the least able children, but it's kind of making sure that that doesn't happen and they do work with other children as well. (Katie, class teacher)

It was clear through discussion with staff, too, that many of them are aware, on a moment-by-moment basis, of the impact their teaching is having on different sections of their class.

> I've got a few children in the class with speech and language problems, so to make sure they were all listening, instead of saying the question once I might say it two or three times to kind of make sure I have got their attention. (Katie, class teacher)

> I'm aware sometimes that when I'm talking I try to talk in a way that all of them will understand. I think that's because of language and obviously some of them, or most of them have English as a Second Language. (Vanessa, class teacher)

For the staff at Bangabandhu, inclusion is about all pupils, not just about focusing on those with a readily definable learning difficulty.

> I think also by having open-ended tasks it means that a child like that [having trouble writing] can take part in the lesson. And it's also like having high expectations of the children, so the more able children know that they've got to do more work and it's got to be of a high standard and it's kind of getting that across to them. It's like making sure everyone does their best. (Katie, class teacher)

# 5 Valued, varied, challenging, relevant?

It appears as if the Bangabandhu community is working hard at achieving a supportive learning culture. It does attempt to break down disabling barriers, there is a good deal of open communication, individuals and groups usually operate with self-control, and full participation and access are generally being sought for all. In order to understand the processes more fully, however, we need to consider the next level of evidence.

# ◯ Activity 5.6   Seeing inclusive practice

In this activity you will watch the rest of Band A, part 1, of the video. First, read the following list carefully and then watch video pages 18 to 105 of 'A day in the journey of Bangabandhu' on the video, looking for examples of inclusive practice. When you have finished watching the video use the list as headings to note down examples.

positive role models

secure pupils

valued pupils

active listening and communication with pupils

varied teaching approaches

varied materials

varied tasks

varied grouping

varied equipment

challenging learning tasks

appropriate learning tasks

focus through relevance

motivation through relevance

assessment in context of experience

clear feedback

After making your list, you may find it useful to watch the video again and/or talk about the practices you observed with someone else who has seen it and then revise your list.

In the rest of this section we describe what we witnessed during our visits to Bangabandhu School. This description will include many of the items you will have noted from the video, as well as some that were not included in the footage.

## Positive role models

Bangabandhu has many positive role models. There are many women in positions of authority. Many of the school's support staff come from the local community. This does not mean everything is representative, however. Staff are very much aware that, to date (2003), there have never been any senior managers or class teachers from the local Bangladeshi community, and they make it clear that they believe there ought to be.

There is a sizeable proportion of staff from the local community, however. Support teachers, classroom teaching assistants, midday supervisors, early education support officers, a bilingual instructor and individual teaching assistants are all drawn from Bangabandhu's local community. There are no staff who are disabled, but the new staff facilities will attempt to maximize accessibility in a similar manner to the rest of the school.

> We've worked very hard on building up a workforce to reflect the community; I would expect to see that, as it's beginning to reflect a much closer match between the, the ethnic mix of our teachers reflecting the local community. And that's starting to happen, but we're not there yet. One of the areas that I'd like to see growing is I'd like to see more disabled teachers working in the Borough. So we've got a long way to go, there are a lot of things in place, in five years' time, I hope to see even more of those in place, and even more schools confident that they can adapt and meet the needs of their community. In its great diversity.
>
> *(Helen Jenner, LEA inclusion officer, E243 video, Band A, video*
> *pages 150–2)*

## Secure and valued pupils

Examples of concern for the welfare of pupils and with making them feel secure were relatively common, from the provision of fruit in class, to teachers discussing whether pupils had eaten breakfast or whether they were wearing warm enough clothing. There were plenty of examples of pupils who achieved less well academically having the confidence to ask questions and express opinions. Staff often referred to their desire to make pupils feel safe and secure.

We saw occasions, and you may have identified some on the video, when pupils were not paid the attention they might have been, or when their requests were turned down. There were examples, too, of some pupils being called upon far more often than others. In one lesson we attended, there was a particular tendency, for example, to let boys answer the questions. However, generally, all pupils' contributions to lessons that we observed were greeted with encouragement and respect. Pupils were made to feel as if they and their ideas were valued, and many obviously felt pride in their own contributions. Staff paid attention to pupils' wishes too, and there was evidence of a concern to reflect the child's personal life in school life. There was occasionally evidence that the views of the child were sought with regard to how they learn and would like to be taught (for example, the visually-impaired pupil helping to improve the mathematics learning materials mentioned in Section 4), and with regard to the social life of the school, but this did not seem to be a priority.

## Varied teaching approaches, materials and tasks

A variety of teaching approaches were used in the classes, and to a certain degree we saw varied materials being used and tasks being carried out. Certainly this was the case in the reception class where pupils were involved in the office area, marble number runs, cooking, using a computer, reading books, and contributing to wall charts and to a whiteboard session.

Before continuing with our description of the school's practices, let us consider the classroom activities in more detail.

## ◯ Activity 5.7   Classroom watching

Watch Band A, part 3, of the video, 'A day in the journey of Bangabandhu continued' (video pages 153–70). Examine the lesson and the supporting commentary and consider the different teaching approaches, varied materials and tasks on display. To what degree and in what ways do you feel that the efforts being made encourage the inclusion of all pupils?

This exercise is a direct rehearsal of the skills you will need in TMA 03.

This video sequence contains examples of class work, one-to-one work and group work. There are also different presentations of the same task, role play, visual representation, discussion, reading, talking and listening tasks and writing tasks. You may have noted the team teaching in operation and also the discussion of forms of texts, scaffolding, scribing and collaboration.

In the numeracy and literacy hours that we observed we might have expected slightly more evidence of differentiation of materials and tasks. As is often the way with these formalized hours, the differentiation tended to be based on setting, with each group using the same theory to carry out similar applications at a different level of complexity. This is an issue that we will discuss further in Units 8 and 13, and was one which the staff did touch on, voicing concern at the need to make sure that tasks and materials were varied according to need.

I think with him [a boy with cerebral palsy] you do have to sort of modify your resources and your activities. For example, I'm not too sure about his sight: we don't think he can see very well far away, so things that we do have, for example, need to be a lot brighter, a lot bigger, very tactile. So, for example, when we're doing counting activities with numbers it's got to be things that he can grip: so not very slippery things, but also things that he can touch. He likes to put things in his mouth as well – I think it's just an extra sense for him – so things that are very tactile and very bright. (Sarah, class teacher)

## Varied groupings

We observed a variety of different forms of grouping, even within sessions that were setted by perceived or measured ability. Setting was used for part of the day only. Staff commented that pupils often did the work being done in other sets when it was appropriate to their learning needs. Within the setted sessions, occasionally pupils worked with pupils from other sets. The staff claimed that they were on the lookout to direct individual pupils to appropriate tasks regardless of their set.

Generally speaking, groups involved boys and girls working together and the staff encouraged this. Group size and membership changed throughout lessons too, although pupils working with a support teacher tended to work in a cluster in the class. As you saw on the video, pupils would work on their own, in pairs, in threes, in larger groups and as a class, according to the purpose of that part of the lesson as defined by the class teacher.

## Varied equipment

There was a variety of equipment in the school, intended to enable physical, social and cognitive access. For example, there was use of gaiters for leg support, wheelchairs, large-key keyboards, soft-edged sports equipment, PECS cards, 'disabled' toilets, and adapted chairs. Whether the use of this equipment always facilitated participation is open to question, of course. For example, if a child has to spend five minutes of a twenty-minute play session having their gaiters put on, is their participation being facilitated by the equipment or restricted, or could the blame for any reduced access be placed on the time limitations of the curriculum? Having said this, in the context of the classes we saw there were genuine attempts to use equipment in a non-invasive and supportive manner to encourage access.

## Challenging, appropriate and relevant learning tasks

A number of staff highlighted the restrictions placed upon them by the national curriculum, mentioning that it created time pressures and imposed requirements that made it hard for subject matter to be made relevant to pupils' experiences. In the literacy session we observed, the class was reading about Icarus, and during the numeracy session they were studying percentages. We had discussions with staff about the relevance of Greek myths to the children, and whether myths from other cultures would have more immediacy. Equally, we talked about the immediate relevance of percentages to children in year 5.

One member of staff pointed out that in many ways the lack of flexibility in what they could teach had enhanced the delivery of material. He pointed out that whereas previously he had spent hours deciding what to teach before thinking about how to do it, now he just got on with finding ways to maximize the learning of the material by all the pupils. The staff tried to draw upon the life experiences of their pupils, searching for areas of relevance to motivate and focus the pupils within the prescribed subjects. The literacy lesson focused very much on the relationship between a father and son and how their personal feelings got in the way of decent communication. The numeracy lesson focused on the purchasing of stamps and how many would be needed for particular letters. The pupils had physical examples of white-paper stamps to make the exercise more tangible.

## Assessment and feedback

Assessment and feedback were made in relation to learning objectives that had been clearly stated at the start of each lesson. Pupils followed a school policy of using learning intentions as the heading for their work too, and this was then referred back to in the marking. All staff were involved in this marking process, which was seen as a means of general communication about the learning that was taking place.

> So we just write little post-it notes and then that helps us, just to know where everybody is, what stage the children are at, but we do have discussions afterwards on you know ... pupils you know who significantly done well or have concerns with. (Sarah, class teacher)

Feedback was seen to take place within the context of the individual pupil's own levels of achievement, too. For example, when a teacher commented on three very different pieces of poetry, demonstrating three different levels of complexity, by three pupils in the same class, her comments all began with a similar supportive message of congratulation. It was clear that staff felt that supportive assessment and feedback in both spoken and written communications was of the utmost importance.

**Example A**

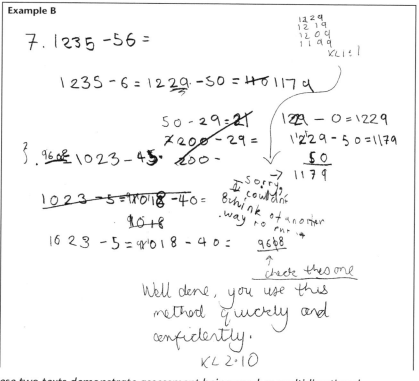

I helped do the copying as Nahima had lost her glasses

Kay 1:4

<u>Similes and Metaphors.</u>

The wind was a Lawe dast of claws

The moon was a wate as a pis of a papa

The trees were like gayent vegtebls

The road was laygk a Blac stret. Layn.

**Example B**

7. 1235 - 56 =

1235 - 6 = 1229 - 50 = 1179

50 - 29 = 21
200 - 29 =
200 -

3. 960 1023 - 45. 

1023 - 5 = 1018 - 40 =
90 + 8
16 23 - 5 = 9018 - 40 = 9608

1229 - 0 = 1229
1229 - 50 = 1179
50
1179

I'm sorry, I couldn't think of another way to put it.

check this one

1229
1219
1209
1199
KL 1:1

Well done, you use this method quickly and confidently.

KL 2:10

These two texts demonstrate assessment being used as multidirectional communication. On them we can see comments made by pupils, support staff and class teachers. Example A shows communication about events within lessons and Example B deals with personal understanding of material.

## Inclusive practice in action

You have now had the opportunity to look at Bangabandhu, a school aspiring to inclusive practice. The last activity in this unit is intended to encourage you to test out your perspectives on the complexities that schools face daily.

# Activity 5.8   So, what would you do?

In this activity you will consider what you would do so as to demonstrate inclusive practice in action. Read the following two scenarios and make notes on the questions.

This activity will help you with TMA 02.

### Scenario 1

An eight year old who has had only six months of schooling arrives in the school. This child demonstrates great interest in the activities taking place in the reception class. The LEA does not approve of pupils being outside age-appropriate classes. What are the risks of placing the child in the reception class? How could you go about minimizing the risks of placing the child there? How could you adapt the age-appropriate class to include activities for this eight year old? What are the risks of this adaptation?

### Scenario 2

Organizational problems have delayed the arrival of a wheelchair to transport a new pupil from the school bus into the school. There is a toddler's pushchair to hand. Will you use the pushchair to transport the pupil? Should the pupil's right to be treated in a manner that does not demean them take precedence over their right to be in school? Or is transportation in this manner more damaging than a delayed entry into the classroom and school community?

*Scenario 1*

We felt that the school should not feel in any way constrained by LEA directives if this would go against the best interests of the pupil. If the pupil was placed within the reception class there is, however, a risk of them being excluded from their age peers. If, however, activities which interest the child are feasible only with a younger group, then they should not be stopped from carrying them out.

There is no reason why other pupils should not move between age groups too. Maybe the school could encourage this as a way of overcoming any sense of isolation the eight year old might feel. This approach could have a wide number of educational uses, such as mentoring or a collaborative art project.

It is also very probable that many reception age-appropriate activities could be included in the eight-year-old class as part of the curriculum. For example, an interest in using the marble run could be built into a project on the different levels of friction caused by different materials. With an open and sensitive approach, there should be no risks.

*Scenario 2*

We felt that the pupil might attend the school as a matter of priority. The school might apologize to the pupil and make it a matter of urgency that the correct equipment is acquired. The pupil might be involved in discussion about how best to minimize the demeaning nature of the act. It might be that the school arranges for classes to examine issues of access in their local area.

# 6 Conclusion

The history of the funding of education in England has resulted in great unevenness in the degree of inclusion in different LEAs and different schools. Under the 1981 Education Act LEAs have statutory responsibility for 'special educational needs'. Under the government's 1999 Fair Funding initiative, however, spending on those needs can be devolved to individual schools.

Bangabandhu School, in the London Borough of Tower Hamlets, is one example of a school that is attempting to work in an inclusive manner. It expresses a commitment to inclusive practice and demonstrates many examples of that practice in action. Bangabandhu has flexibility in management, communication, rules and practices as well as clearly understood and shared values. It has teachers and support staff who work as teams and try to assess the impact of their actions on a moment-by-moment basis.

The school acknowledges the constraints placed upon it by the wider education system and attempts to find space for staff and pupils within those constraints. There is a sense of a community whose members feel they are involved with each other in a supportive, open and yet challenging environment, and that this community has clear links with the wider community that it serves. The school appears to care for pupils, to respect and listen to them, and the pupils' behaviour seems to reflect both this and the positive collaborative behaviour of the staff around them. Most impressive of all, Bangabandhu School seems to genuinely appreciate that there is still much to learn.

## References

Audit Commission (2002) *Special Educational Needs: a mainstream issue*, London, Audit Commission. Available at: http://www.audit-commission.gov.uk [accessed 17 June 2003].

Blamires, M. (1999) 'Universal design for learning: re-establishing differentiation as part of the inclusion agenda?', *Support for Learning*, **14**(4), pp. 158–63.

Department for Education and Employment (DfEE) (1997) *Excellence for All Children: meeting special educational needs*, London, HMSO (Green Paper).

Department for Education and Employment (DfEE) (2000) *The Role of the Local Education Authority in School Education*, London, DfEE. Available from: http://www.dfee.gov.uk/learole/policypaper/ [accessed 17 June 2003].

Department for Education and Skills (DfES) (2002) *Distribution of Resources to Support Inclusion: draft guidance*, London, DfES. Available from: http://www.dfes.gov.uk/sen/documents/SENFUND22JUNE.htm [accessed 9 April 2003].

Downes, P. (2003) 'Funding reform brings clarity, more money and some disappointment', *Governors News*, National Association of Governors and Managers, February, p. 2.

Dyson, A., Millward, A., Crowther, D., Elliott, J. and Hall, I. (2002) *Decision Making and Provision within the Framework of the SEN Code of Practice*, Research Report No. 248, London, DfES.

Fletcher-Campbell, F. (2002) 'The financing of special education: lessons from Europe', *Support for Learning*, **17**(1), pp. 19–22.

Goacher, B., Evans, J., Welton, J. and Wedell, K. (1988) *Policy and Provision for Special Educational Needs: implementing the 1981 Education Act*, London, Cassell.

Gray, P. (2002) 'Custodians of entitlement or agents of dependence? SEN support services in English LEAs in the context of greater delegation of funding to schools', *Support for Learning*, **17**(1), pp. 5–8.

Lindsay, G. and Dockrell, J. (2002) 'Meeting the needs of children with speech and language communication needs: a critical perspective on inclusion and collaboration', *Child Language Teaching and Therapy*, **18**(2), pp. 91–101.

Ofsted (1998) *Inspection of Tower Hamlets Local Education Authority*, London, Ofsted.

Ofsted (2000) Inspection of Tower Hamlets Local Education Authority, London, Ofsted.

Schein, E. (1984) 'Coming to a new awareness of organizational culture', *Sloan Management Review*, **25**.

Thomas, G. (1992) 'Local authorities, special needs, and the status quo', *Support for Learning*, **7**(1), pp. 36–40.

Vincent, C., Evans, J., Lunt, I. and Young, P. (1996) 'Professionals under pressure: the administration of special education in a changing context', *British Educational Research Journal*, **22**(4), pp. 475–91.

# UNIT 6  Visions, definitions and interpretations

*Prepared for the course team by Melanie Nind and Mary Kellett*

## Contents

# 1 Introduction

In Unit 5 you gained some insights into inclusive education in practice. You were also given insights into some of the perspectives of the various stakeholders involved with Bangabandhu School. We now look at the perspectives of academics and disabled writers and their (sometimes more abstract) concepts of inclusive education. You will remember from reading Richard Light's Chapter 12 in Reader 1 that there is not always a happy union between academics and disabled activists. Academics have sometimes been guilty of taking over agendas from the people at the heart of struggles for inclusive education and disability rights. We are certainly guilty in this unit of referencing more work by non-disabled academics and theorists, whose volume of work is greater, than by disabled activists and theorists. Whoever produces it, however, addressing the theory of inclusion is important because, while inclusion is about people and action, it is also about ideas. The thinking and vision of others have inspired some of the changes that schools have undertaken to make them more inclusive. The way we think about inclusion issues can also change the way we see ourselves and how others see us, as Vic Finkelstein illustrates:

> 'You want to change the world?' The questioner asked with an expression of incredulity. I hesitated. Should I answer truthfully or back away as we so often did in public? We were attending a Central Television feedback meeting at a very early stage in the presentation of the Sunday morning LINK programmes. I had argued the case for a clear and open platform for the social interpretation of disability. We were not just pressing our case for the able-bodied world to accept us, to be more caring and make adjustments for our 'needs', but suggesting that the able-bodied world had to change – it was disabling us. 'Yes' I replied after a moment. 'We want to change the world' and with this I changed myself, my public identity, from a passive-dependent user of care services to an active citizen expressing my fundamental human right to have an impact on the world in which I live.
>
> *(Finkelstein, 1996)*

Reading the theoretical work and hearing the arguments of others can help us to develop our own position; as authors of the course we are aware of this process in our own development. We hope that reading the material in this unit will help you develop your own perspectives on what inclusive education is and should be. We may learn most about inclusive education by getting on and doing it, as Norman Kunc has argued (in Ballard, 1995, p. 10), but we are not all in a position to do this. Instead, or additionally, we can draw on others' lived experiences of inclusion/exclusion, and on their thinking, to provide key concepts and stimulate reflection and discussion.

## Learning outcomes

By the end of this unit you will:

- understand that thinking about inclusive education is context-bound, evolving and varied;
- be able to think about inclusive education as a social construct;
- be able to know about a range of different visions, definitions and interpretations of what constitutes inclusive education;
- be able to identify common ground and areas of contention in concepts of inclusive education;
- be able to critically discuss the different dimensions of inclusive education – the values dimension, policy dimension, organizational dimension, curriculum dimension and teaching and learning dimension;
- begin to critique and evaluate different perspectives;
- develop your own position on what constitutes inclusive education.

## Resources for this unit

In the course of your study of this unit we ask you to read the following chapters from Reader 1:

- Chapter 6, 'The politics of education for all', by Len Barton.
- Chapter 21, 'Viewing inclusion from a distance: gaining perspective from comparative study' by Tony Booth.

# 2   What is inclusive education?

## Inclusive education and contexts

In Unit 3 you saw how disability can be understood as a social construct. In this unit you will see how inclusive education is socially constructed too. There is no objective truth or certainty about it (Allan, 2000) – it is contextual. This means, as Jenny Corbett (1999, p. 53) observes, that 'what counts as inclusive in one context may be seen as highly exclusive in another'. In the UK inclusive education tends to be focused primarily around disability and disaffection, within the wider context of gender, ethnicity, poverty and so on. In contrast, in many countries below the equator, which hold the majority of the world's population but control the minority of the world's wealth, inclusive education is primarily aimed at bringing primary education to everyone. Hazel Bines reflects on this in the light of her journey through teaching and teacher training in the UK to working as an education advisor in Pakistan:

> So what do inclusion and policy mean to me now? In Pakistan they include ensuring access to education for the half of Pakistan's children who do not, or cannot, attend school. And developing education for girls in particular, and for disadvantaged children, many of whose families depend on their working income.

*(Bines, 2001, p. 93)*

## Activity 6.1   From a distance

Now read Chapter 21, 'Viewing inclusion from a distance: gaining perspective from comparative study', by Tony Booth in Reader 1. As you read, jot down the different aspects of context that make a difference to how inclusion is understood.

Next, use the method from comparative study of 'making the strange familiar and the familiar strange'. Imagine you are from a different place in the world, or a different time, giving you different resources and expectations: what might you see in a school you know that you might see as inclusionary or exclusionary?

This is useful practice for exploring scenarios in TMA 02.

## Historical contexts

As you will have seen, inclusive education is constructed in context in terms of its place in history as well as geography and politics. What we understand as good inclusive education today may be regarded as misguided by future generations. Jenny Corbett (1997) comments on this, arguing that in recent history 'we have moved on from the "dump and hope" model of inclusion, in which placement alone is the criterion for success' (p. 58), to a genuine concern with inclusive teaching and learning. Similarly, Mel Ainscow (2000), as the former head of a special school, comments on changes, this time in his own thinking. He describes how in the 1980s he 'moved from being concerned with particular children to being concerned with contexts' (p. 39). He explains how his involvement with school effectiveness and then school improvement shifted his focus on to schools and to what was and wasn't working.

The idea of inclusive education as an emerging and ongoing project is an important theme in this unit. It is important for us to recognize that thinking about inclusive education has not just emerged from nowhere. There are roots in history and for individuals in their own personal journeys. In *The Making of the Inclusive School*, Gary Thomas, David Walker and Julie Webb (1998, p. 4) describe the journey towards inclusive education in one local education authority. In more general terms they also describe a wider journey in which inclusion has come to the forefront of thinking. They identify the coming together of three key developments in history as crucial to this:

1   'the world-wide push for civil rights', which is liberating disabled people 'to give voice to their anger about the stigma, degradation and curricular and social limits imposed by the segregated education to which they had been subjected';

2   'evidence about the surprising lack of success of the segregated system', and

3   evidence 'that the special system selected disproportionately children from ethnic minorities and children from lower socio-economic groups'.

## Controversies

Perspectives on inclusive education are not just evolving – they are also varied. Peter Clough comments:

> The term 'inclusive education' has itself come to mean many different things which can in itself create confusion for students in this area. It is in fact a contestable term used to different effect by politicians, bureaucrats and academics. 'Inclusion' is not a single *movement*; it is made up of many strong currents of belief, many different local struggles and a myriad forms of practice.
>
> (Clough, 2000, p. 6)

We need to remember that there are fashions with language and that sometimes education authorities have simply changed the word 'integration' to 'inclusion' on their policy documents as a means of keeping up with the times. While we may not seek one tidy definition of inclusion, we do need a strong enough conceptual framework to evaluate the extent to which it is happening. Without this, we are vulnerable to claims that 'inclusion doesn't work' when it may never really have been properly attempted. We are faced with the challenge of understanding where different arguments about inclusive education inform and complement each other and where there are tensions. Clough maintains that there tends to be agreement at the moral stage of defining inclusive education, but that when we move on to enacting inclusive practice 'what was intended to be a uniform platform may disintegrate into more fragmented demands' (2000, p. 6). In this unit you will see differences even at the philosophical level.

# 3  Boundaries to inclusion

## Who is inclusive education about?

Some concepts of inclusive education can be clustered together on the basis of their concern with the boundaries around it – who it does and does not concern and what it is and is not about. First, we need to ask who is included in inclusive education.

Rosenthal (2001) is clear about his view of who and what inclusion involves beyond the traditional notion of 'special educational need':

> I intend 'inclusion' to mean involving and recognising the broad universe of differences that pupils present; of gender, of ethnicity, of cultural heritage, of religion, of languages and of sexuality.
>
> *(Rosenthal, 2001, p. 386)*

This is in keeping with the majority of the definitions of inclusion that stress that it is about all learners. As Tony Booth explains, in Chapter 21 of Reader 1:

> Learners with impairments and others categorised as 'having special educational needs' are only some of those subjected to exclusionary pressures. It is counterproductive to tie a notion of inclusive education to only some of the learners vulnerable to marginalisation. The participation of real learners, who all have multiple group membership, requires schools that are responsive to all aspects of learner diversity.
>
> *(Booth, Reader 1, Chapter 21, p. 254)*

One of the important elements in discourses of inclusive education is the emphasis on learning contexts rather than learners themselves as the 'problem'. This has allowed a shift away from thinking about learners with impairments as distinct from other learners who may experience barriers to learning related to a whole range of other disabling and disadvantaging processes. While it is disabled people who have spoken out about their particular experiences of segregation in special schools and of statementing, by identifying their oppression they have identified themselves as sharing some common ground with other oppressed groups.

From 1997, the Government took up the notion of inclusive education addressing all kinds of diversity. But there is an interesting twist here in the way national policy has been refocused back on groups of learners as 'inclusion groups'. The Ofsted guidance for inspectors and schools, for instance, makes clear that educational inclusion is about different groups of pupils, that is, 'any or all of':

- girls and boys;

- minority ethnic and faith groups, Travellers, asylum seekers and refugees;

- pupils who need support to learn English as an additional language (EAL);

- pupils with special educational needs;

- gifted and talented pupils;

- children 'looked after' by the local authority;

- other children, such as sick children; young carers; those children from families under stress; pregnant school girls and teenage mothers; and any pupils who are at risk of disaffection and exclusion.

*(Ofsted, 2002)*

Whilst this document and much academic literature are specific in unpacking what is meant by 'all learners', there are some mixed messages in the various discussions about who and what inclusion is about. On the one hand there is an official rhetoric that this is about all learners and, on the other, there is a continual tendency to revert back to focusing on learners whose barriers to participation relate to learning difficulties or impairments. We ourselves are guilty of this!

Our different journeys to our interest in inclusive education reflect our different histories and influence the communities of learners we focus on. Many proponents of inclusive education come via a history in which they were part of the special education system. This might be as a 'special school survivor', or it may be as a professional working within the arena of 'special educational needs provision'. It is partly because of the experiences of the course team that this course about inclusive education dwells frequently on disabled children and children with learning difficulties. We also focus on these groups, though, because of the role disabled activists and academics have played in highlighting their discrimination and segregation in building a voice for inclusion.

The *International Journal of Inclusive Education* has been influential in maintaining a broad spectrum of learners in its papers on inclusive education. Articles on Black pupils failed by the school; class, gender and education; responding to diversity in organizational life; adjusted school environments; and the cost of school exclusion illustrate the broad remit of inclusive education. This diverse list of topics also reminds us that many visions of inclusion are about processes more than individuals.

A clear message to come from the various discourses within inclusive education is that learners do not fit into discrete categories, each requiring separate and particular education. Learners are diverse and have multiple identities, but they have common rights and needs to learn. Activists and academics remind us of this and that the implication is that 'all teachers are responsible ... for all children' (Mittler, 2000a, p. 11).

*Symbol used on Parents for Inclusion's P.A.T.H. (Planning Alternative Tomorrows with Hope) poster*

 ## Activity 6.2   Real people; real experiences

Think about pupils who might be vulnerable to being excluded from participation and learning in school. This might be long or short-term. Think about the barriers to their participation and learning. Try to think in terms of real people. Have you been in this situation? Can you move outside of the 'boxes' of categories of learners?

This exercise is good for reminding us that inclusive education is not just about 'other' people. We remembered incidents when we were vulnerable to exclusion:

- being the only working-class child from a council estate in a grammar school meant never really belonging;
- not being able to afford to go on the school trip;
- not being able to stay for after-school activities because of being needed at home by a disabled mum;
- being picked on for having an Irish name.

Of course, these experiences cannot be equated with the institutional discrimination and segregation experienced by disabled people/pupils, but they do illustrate shared and individual experiences of discrimination and marginalization.

## Inclusion or integration?

One of the challenges for you as a student of inclusive education is to understand the distinction between integration and inclusion. This is made all the more challenging by some documents (particularly those of the Government) using the two terms interchangeably. In addition, there is no universal agreement on how the concepts are different. Tony Booth, for instance, is unusual in seeing both integration and inclusion as being about 'the process of increasing the participation in their schools and communities of people subjected to exclusionary pressures and practices' (Booth, 1995, p. 101). However, there is something of a consensus – enough to provide 'signposts in the fog' (Mittler, 2000a, p. 10). The following quotations illustrate the kinds of agreement we can find in the literature:

> The change from integration to inclusion is much more than a fashionable change in politically correct semantics … *Integration* involves preparing pupils for placement in ordinary schools … The pupil must adapt to the school and there is no necessary assumption that the school will change to accommodate a greater diversity of pupils … *Inclusion* implies a radical reform of the school in terms of curriculum, assessment, pedagogy and grouping of pupils.
>
> *(Mittler, 2000a, p. 10)*

> Inclusive [education] is about learning to live with one another … not about assimilation in which a process of accommodation leaves the school remaining essentially unchanged …
>
> *(Barton, Reader 1, Chapter 6, p. 60)*

> [Integration means] Young people with special educational needs being placed in mainstream provision with some adaptations and resources but on condition that the young person can fit in with pre-existing structures, attitudes and an unaltered environment. [Inclusion means] Young people with special educational needs being placed in mainstream provision, where there is a commitment to removing all barriers to the full participation of each child as a valued, unique individual.
>
> *(Alliance for Inclusive Education, 2002)*

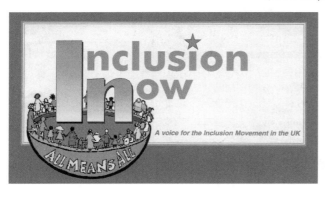

We can see here how inclusion has developed as a concept in contrast to integration. It is frequently understood in terms of how it goes further than integration, or operates in fundamentally different ways from integration. The term is sometimes used in an attempt to encapsulate a fullness of inclusion and genuine participation (Farrell, 2001). The definition of inclusive education adopted by the Alliance for Inclusive Education (in April 2000) stresses equality and participation as well as location:

> Inclusive education enables all students to fully participate in any mainstream early years provision, school, college or university. Inclusive education provision has training and resources aimed at fostering every student's equality and participation in all aspects of the learning community.
>
> *(Alliance for Inclusive Education, 2001)*

*Based on Inclusion Network, Marsha Forest Centre, 2003.*

Integration is often criticized, with hindsight, for two major faults that inclusion seeks to address. First, integration is linked with notions of readiness, focusing on whether the learner has 'the necessary skills and attributes to literally "fit into" the mainstream school' (Blamires, 1999, p. 158). This is a very one-way model and does not ask what the school is doing to ready itself to match the requirements of the learner. Inclusion is more concerned with the changes that the schools can make. Preoccupation with pupils 'fitting in' is criticized as a kind of assimilationist thinking. It treats difference as something to be minimized, rather than valued – the less different someone seems, the better they will fit the mainstream situation. In contrast, as we shall explore further later in this unit, inclusive education involves treating difference as welcome and ordinary.

Second, integration is criticized for having been 'too narrowly interpreted as placement' (Rouse and Florian, 1997, p. 325). That is, it has focused on where a learner is educated rather than the quality of learning and participation that goes on there. It has focused on moving where the learner (usually with 'special educational needs') is located, and not on addressing barriers to learning and participation. Inclusive education is largely seen as being about both placement and participation, though the relative importance placed on each varies across commentators.

Michael Oliver (1996) pulls out a key difference underpinning some of these issues of who does the changing and how much participation can be expected. Integration (a concept usually reserved for disabled pupils rather than for other areas of diversity) is predominantly on non-disabled people's terms. Inclusion, in contrast, is on disabled people's terms. As we have discussed in earlier units, to be given something by those in power, or to have to earn it, is very different from claiming something as a right. In integration a placement in an ordinary school may be offered or worked for and always vulnerable, whereas in inclusion a meaningful place in an ordinary school would be an entitlement.

 # Activity 6.3   How inclusive?

Look at the following examples. Reflect on the distinctions that may mean that some of these seem to you to be much more inclusive than others.

This exercise will help to prepare you for the assignments by helping you to clarify your own understandings.

Jack has autism. He attends a special school, but joins a local mainstream primary school for two afternoons a week for PE and music. Once a term his class in the special school and his class in the mainstream school get together for a fun day, performance or special event.

Bharti has Down's syndrome. She attends a mainstream school and a teacher from the learning support service works alongside her teacher for some of her lessons. The support teacher works with Bharti and other children in small groups and plans schemes of work with Bharti's regular teacher.

Spencer has multi-sensory impairment. He will be joining the nursery next term. A teacher and nursery nurse have made several home visits to get to know Spencer in his familiar surroundings. They have discussed with his mum the kinds of things that will help him to settle in to the nursery and the kinds of activities that he will enjoy participating in.

Mark attends a behavioural support unit. The unit is part of a mainstream school. It is situated in a temporary classroom in the playground. The unit is staffed by specialist teachers, who have their own mini-staffroom and office in the temporary building.

Mary lives with her family on a permanent site for Travellers. She attends school with no support. She enjoys helping with the 'little ones' and sits quietly in lessons. She rarely engages with the curriculum and chooses not to take part in class discussions. Her teachers see her as no different from the other children.

Our response to this activity was that occasional integration better describes Jack and Mark's situation. They are not seen as rightful members of an ordinary school or as the responsibility of everyone in the school. The school staff working with Bharti and Spencer, in contrast, are taking responsibility for their inclusion rather than leaving this to specialists or to the children themselves to make the adjustments needed to fit in. For Mary, the curriculum is excluding – it is not a caring or inclusive curriculum and her participation is not valued.

## Inclusion and exclusion

You may have noted the concern of Tony Booth and others with 'people subjected to exclusionary pressures and practices'. There is an important connection being made here between inclusion and exclusion. Booth (1996) has connected the process of increasing participation with 'the process of decreasing exclusionary pressures'. Moreover, he has argued that attempting to increase participation without attempting to decrease exclusionary pressures is self-defeating. He explains:

> I define inclusion in education in terms of two linked processes. It is the process of increasing the participation of learners in and reducing their exclusion from the curricula, cultures and communities of neighbourhood mainstream centres of learning. My definition recognises the reality of exclusionary pressures in education and the

need to identify and counter them, if the participation of learners is to be increased. I have begun to call this project 'inclusion/exclusion'.

*(Booth, Reader 1, Chapter 21, p. 253)*

This may seem like common sense, or even stating the obvious. We have to remember, however, that the discourses of inclusion and exclusion have often been kept apart. This is because, until disabled activists raised the profile of disabled pupils as excluded pupils, 'inclusion' and 'exclusion' have largely been applied to different populations. There is a history of talking about integrating and then including disabled pupils and pupils with learning difficulties, and a history of talking about the exclusion of 'pupils with emotional and behavioural difficulties'. From this starting point, the understanding of a linked inclusion/exclusion process is a conceptual development.

Some inclusionists, such as Len Barton and Micheline Mason, have raised awareness of how exclusion disempowers people. Unless there is inclusion, some people are cast as 'other and outside of a "normal" frame of reference' (Barton, 1997, p. 232). Excluded people are shut out from the ordinary experiences that give us value and power; this has been the case for disabled pupils in special schools. From this viewpoint, segregated special schools have no role to play in an inclusive education system.

## Between inclusion and exclusion

In some thinking about inclusive education inclusion and exclusion are presented as opposites of each other, or as at extreme ends of a continuum. Jenny Corbett (1997), however, has questioned the usefulness of this because it 'fails to reflect the various stages of in-between-ness' that exist in real contexts (p. 56). Corbett reminds us of compromises and individual preferences that are less tidy than the usual split between one extreme and another. She raises the issues of parents and other stakeholders who want neither extreme, but rather some kind of best deal in difficult circumstances. An example of the best deal might be going to the nearest accessible ordinary school, even if this isn't the nearest school *per se*. This raises for us the question of when such a messy compromise, or mixture of inclusion and exclusion, would become something that we would feel comfortable describing as inclusive education, or whether indeed we should just maintain a concept of inclusion as something much more fluid.

Between inclusion and exclusion can also feel like an uncomfortable place to be. Some of you will work in special schools or have children in special schools and feel a loyalty to them. This may increase as a defensive feeling as you pursue the course, or you may feel a sense of contradiction of the kind Michael Oliver describes:

> I give the introductory lecture to visiting Dutch students
> and I am conscious that I want the lecture to say that

special education is bad and therefore all of you are oppressors and there is a sense in which I actually believe that. That is not a very helpful thing to tell students on their first day on a course. One has to say things which do justice to the complexities and which don't denigrate the very real commitments which lots of people put into their professional practice, not simply to build careers and pay their mortgages but because they are genuinely committed to working for the children in their schools. I think inevitably all we can do is live with those contradictions.

*(Oliver, 2000a, p. 114)*

## Summary

Different writers and thinkers on inclusive education draw different limits around the concept. Distinctions are frequently made between inclusion and integration. These are based on qualitative differences in how a school responds to diversity. There is some consensus that the focus for inclusion must be on all learners. This is sometimes translated into the broad range of learners who may be vulnerable to exclusion or marginalization by systems and people. The question of when a school has done enough to be defined as inclusive is hotly debated.

# 4  Journeys to inclusion – an ongoing process

I have a transformative approach to inclusion which involves asking how can we actually transform the education system, such that it is more capable of developing its capacity to reach out to all learners in a way which suggests it is an ever ongoing process that never ends in that sense.

*(Ainscow, 2000, p. 41)*

Inclusion/exclusion is an unending project, applying to all learners who are vulnerable to exclusion from their local schools and to the construction of an education system that recognises and is responsive to learner diversity within common groups.

*(Booth, Reader 1, Chapter 21, p. 253)*

My own research, involving listening to pupils' accounts of mainstreaming, suggests that inclusion is never complete, but always in process, which contrasts with the static picture that is often presented of inclusion being *done* to individuals.

*(Allan, 2000, p. 43)*

The quotations above come from three writers in inclusive education, Mel Ainscow, Tony Booth and Julie Allan, who have very different backgrounds and conceptual frameworks, but nonetheless agree on the notion of a journey in inclusion.

## An active process

These writers on inclusive education might have different ideas about how the process of inclusion happens and who is central to it, but they hold in common the view that inclusive education is an active *process*. It is something that people work towards – continually strive for.

## Activity 6.4   A never-ending journey

Take a few minutes to reflect back on Bangabandhu School in Unit 5. What did you learn about this school's process of change? Would the idea of inclusive education as a never-ending journey fit with the perspectives of the various stakeholders involved?

Mike Blamires (1999) contends that whether inclusion is an event or a process depends on a school's starting place and the amount of change needed. It follows that those who envision inclusive education as a process or a journey imagine that much change is needed. This might be change in terms of whole systems, or change at a school or classroom level. Or it may be about all of these. Len Barton (1998), who is chairperson of Disability Equality in Education, for instance, looks to change on a range of levels. He argues that inclusive education is more than access into mainstream school and ending unacceptable segregation. For him it is a process in which a whole range of systems have to change, including physical factors, curriculum aspects, expectations, teaching styles and leadership roles. You will read more from Barton later in the unit.

## A process with changing ideas at the heart

Some writers are very clear about who is central to the process of change. For John Swain this is disabled people who have raised the profile of disabled pupils and illustrated their oppression. Though not writing specifically about inclusive education, Penny Germon notes how, for disabled people, involvement in political struggles is not motivated by altruism:

> We are in this struggle because ultimately we benefit. It is both unreasonable and naïve to expect that we will not be concerned with our own liberation: to the contrary, our own experience of oppression is an *essential* motivating force.

*(Germon, 1999, p. 248)*

Monica Hunter, chairperson of People First (Scotland), is clear why inclusive education is in the interests of disabled people. In a leaflet (undated) from the Alliance for Inclusive Education she argues that:

> Special schools divide children because of the differences they have which they can't do anything about. They stop contacts between children. Special schools lead to ignorance and fear. Going to ordinary schools would let everyone know it's OK to be different and would help disabled people to be treated as people first.

For Mel Ainscow, it is teachers who are at the heart of the process. He writes about his own personal journey in coming to new ideas through reflection on his own practice (Ainscow, 2000). In the UNESCO project, Special Needs in the Classroom (Ainscow, 1994), he and the teachers participating from across the world engaged in a collaborative process of questioning and enhancing practice. They adopted a curriculum view, rather than an individual view, which meant that they saw learners who were experiencing difficulties as providing useful feedback on their classroom practice, rather than as having individual deficits. Responding to this feedback was part of the teachers' role in improving schools and making teaching and learning more effective for everyone involved.

## A process with children at the heart

Julie Allan has taken the less usual step of seeing pupils at the heart of the inclusion process. In Actively Seeking Inclusion (Allan, 1999), she shows how some pupils struggle to be included. She also shows how other pupils assist or interfere in what is never a straightforward process. Through her study of the interactions and opinions of one group of Scottish pupils, we see how being included or excluded, supported or unsupported, was continually oscillating for them. Inclusion of the pupils officially regarded as having 'special educational needs' was in no sense a 'once-and-for-all event' (Allan, 1999, p. 31).

## Transition or transformation

In his keynote address to the International Special Education Congress, Michael Oliver (2000b) described a kind of transition process. He talked about a big shift happening from the special education paradigm or way of thinking and practising, to the inclusive education paradigm, because the special education one was unsustainable. This, he said, was due to its anomalies: being based on a medical rather than an educational view, having systematic bias in patterns of more boys, Black and working-class children in special education, and serving the needs of professionals and other groups of children more than the needs of children in them. He also argued that special education faces demise because of changes beyond education where there are calls for an inclusive society. Lastly, but of no small importance, he talked of the special education paradigm 'being transformed by the dissenting voices of disabled people ourselves: we are writing ourselves into the picture'.

Similarly, Gary Thomas and Andrew Loxley (2001) regard the thinking and practice of inclusive education as being so completely different to that of special education that special education thinking must be broken down, or 'deconstructed', before a new inclusion can be formed. Otherwise the thinking of special education will not so much be a sound platform on which to build the thinking and practice of inclusive education, but instead will undermine it.

Transition can be sudden or gradual, full or partial. While perspectives on inclusive education as a journey are commonplace, we can find great variation in perspectives on what that journey is like. This might be likened to a gradual road, with a gentle incline; a steep and twisting road; an obstacle course; or a step into a different terrain.

## A process of school improvement

In many concepts of inclusive education the emphasis is on systems as much as individuals. This is the position taken by Gary Thomas et al. (1998, p. 19) who stress that 'change has to be systemic as well as individual'. Increasingly, the process of making schools more inclusive is seen as part of a wider process of improving schools. In turn, 'school improvement' is one of the processes through which schools enhance their capacity to respond to an increasing diversity of pupils (Florian et al., 1998).

Proponents of a school improvement perspective focus on how schools currently are, as well as how they want them to be after their journey of improvement. This draws people into pragmatic and technical thinking about what works in inclusive education (Sebba and Sachdev, 1997). This can be seen as less abstract or idealistic than a focus purely on what the elusive end-point of the journey will look like. When the vision of inclusive schools barely resembles schools as they currently are, some people question the whole possibility of reaching the end of the journey. For others, the important thing is setting out on the road of the journey and overcoming obstacles along the way.

A strength of school improvement perspectives is that they draw people away from the traditional search for special techniques for special children and instead focus on practices that work for all children. In this sense school improvement perspectives connect the desire to include all learners with the desire to make schools better places for learning.

Just as some inclusionist thinking is criticized for being too idealistic, some school improvement thinking is criticized for being overly

simplistic. The process of improving schools can be presented as if it is straightforward and linear – a matter of management – when in fact it is a process that is complex and messy – a matter of evolution or revolution. Moreover, school improvement discourses imply that all those involved are equal winners and may underestimate the sense in which, often, some students gain more than others.

## The Index for Inclusion

The *Index for Inclusion* (Booth *et al.*, 2000) is a government sponsored set of materials to 'support schools in a process of inclusive school development' (p. 7). The Index combines a school improvement model with a strong emphasis on an envisioned inclusive ideal. It brings together practical agendas, academic agendas, the campaigning agenda of the Centre for Studies in Inclusive Education, and the government policy agenda of enhancing inclusive practice. The proposed process of inclusive school development involves a planned series of systematic stages:

1   Start a process of becoming familiar with the materials, concepts and methods

2   Find out about the school through self-review and identify some priorities

3   Produce a school development plan that reflects inclusive aims and school priorities

4   Implement a series of developments to support changes towards more inclusive practices, policies and cultures; put priorities into practice

5   Review and monitor progress.

The whole process encouraged by the *Index for Inclusion* involves asking questions and using the answers to those questions to plan and make changes. Questions included in the materials include, for example:

A.1.1.vii)     Does the entrance hall reflect all members of the school community?

A.1.2.viii)    Do students understand that different degrees of conformity to school rules may be expected from different students?

B.1.4.vii)     Are projects concerned with improving the accessibility of the school buildings part of the school curriculum?

C.1.2.iv)      Do curriculum materials reflect the backgrounds and experiences of all learners?

These questions help the staff to know whether there are indicators that various dimensions of inclusive education are in place. Answering yes to the first question would provide support for the indicator that 'Everyone is made to feel welcome' which is part of 'Building community', a feature of an 'Inclusive school culture'. Answering yes to the second question is an indicator that 'Students help each other', also part of building community in an inclusive school culture. The third question is about making buildings accessible as part of 'Developing a school for all' as a feature of 'Producing inclusive policies'. And so on.

▷ # Activity 6.5   Questions to ask

From what you already understand about inclusive education, jot down ten questions that you might ask as part of a school self-review. Note down underneath each question what feature of inclusive education the answer might tell you about.

If you can, compare your questions with those of another student on the course. Have you thought about similar issues? Your questions may have been influenced by the course materials or by your own individual experiences.

You might find it a useful learning tool and revision aid to add to this list of questions as you read further. Thinking in this way will help you to be clear about your developing position, which is assessed in the TMAs.

What are the possible benefits and disadvantages of this kind of school improvement approach?

▶ In Appendix 1 the different indicators given in the *Index for Inclusion* are outlined. We would argue that the discussions that go on among staff about such statements are an important part of the process. Some of these would be more or less relevant depending on the individual school's context. Ongoing evaluation seems to us to be critical to an inclusive approach and would need to be maintained over and above a checklist mentality.

## A process of curriculum change

The early Open University courses that addressed inclusive education (E241 *Special Needs in Education* and E242 *Learning For All*) held a strong position that difficulties in learning arise not from inadequacies in pupils, but from a mismatch between the curriculum and the learner. The important point was, and still is, that it is the curriculum and not the child that is ill fitted and in need of change. This construct of inclusive education stresses a curriculum rather than an individual view. You will see that this is compatible with the social model of disability we discussed in Unit 3.

Some commentators, such as Peter Clough, regard the curriculum as the main vehicle for exclusion and therefore for inclusion. Segregated systems of education are characterized by separate and different curriculam for example, historically, the skills-based or developmental curriculum of old special schools versus the academic curricula of mainstream and the different balance of subjects available in different types of mainstream. It has been argued that the introduction of the national curriculum in England and Wales in 1989 brought all learners together, sharing a common curriculum if not always sharing common spaces in ordinary schools (Lewis, 1995). For some, a curriculum for all is seen as the key to being included – an assertion of their common humanity. Many teachers of children with severe learning difficulties have enjoyed the ways in which they, as well as their learners, have found themselves part of a mainstream framework. Great energies have been put into shaping children to fit the curriculum and adapting the curriculum to meet the needs of children.

Some inclusionists stress the idea that the curriculum should fit the child, but there is a tension in that if this leads to different curricula it also leads to divisions between learners. Wholesale questioning of or resistance to the national curriculum by teachers of 'children with severe learning difficulties' has been negated by a strong desire to be included rather than excluded, following a history of exclusion (Nind, 2002). Nonetheless, a key question remains as to whether this curriculum provides an appropriate umbrella under which to unite (Ware, 1997; Aird, 2001). Will Swann (1992) has highlighted the ways in which the structure of the national curriculum in England and Wales, with its normative key stage assessments, has intensified the distinctions between learners in their classification as failures and successes. Roger Slee (1999) has described what others see as a curriculum for all as the 'curriculum of the dead' and Stephen Ball (1994) as the 'curriculum as museum'. By valuing particular forms of knowledge, he argues, the curriculum fails vast numbers of learners from working-class and minority ethnic backgrounds who are disadvantaged in not being able to make meaningful connections with it.

The relaxing of the national curriculum for some fourteen to nineteen year olds can be seen as offering an alternative framework with options more likely to engage more learners. But this can be criticized too for returning to a situation in which students receive a different kind of education according to their social class and cultural status.

## Summary

In this section we have shown how various definitions of inclusive education share the common ground of inclusion as a change process. How this change happens, who is key to it and what the end product looks like is contested. The definition that Judy Sebba and Mel Ainscow came up with after many attempts represents much current thinking:

> Inclusion describes the process by which a school attempts to respond to all pupils as individuals by reconsidering its curricular organisation and provision. Through this process, the school builds its capacity to

accept all pupils from the local community who wish to attend and, in so doing, reduces the need to exclude pupils.

*(Sebba and Ainscow, 1996, p. 9)*

You should note that the word 'exclude' is used here as the opposite of 'include' and in a broader sense than the common usage associated with exclusion orders or official fixed-term or permanent exclusions.

# 5 Being pragmatic about inclusion

## A practical project

Many concepts of inclusive education emphasize a moral or values position. Few people would argue against inclusive education when inclusion is seen as a democratic or human right. This position tends to place importance on the views of users of education services. The human rights perspective is so important that it is the one we have chosen to end this unit with. First, though, we explore a different stance and look at more pragmatic perspectives on inclusive education. These tend to emphasize the views of service-providers in education.

The school improvement model of inclusive education that we have already addressed is at the forefront of pragmatic perspectives. In focusing on school improvement, proponents are saying that there are practical steps that school staff can take in moving towards inclusion. From this position, inclusion and making better schools are sensible and integrally linked projects with practical actions and down-to-earth benefits for a whole range of pupils; effectiveness is as much a driver and motivator for inclusive education as any concept of rights or social justice. The Centre for Studies in Inclusive Education (CSIE) argue for inclusive education both because it is a human right *and* because it makes good education sense. They maintain that:

1   Research shows children do better, academically and socially, in integrated settings.

2   There is no teaching or care in a segregated school which cannot take place in an ordinary school.

3   Given commitment and support, inclusive education is a more efficient use of educational resources.

*(CSIE, 2002)*

There is support amongst some academics for the perspective that inclusive education is more cost-effective than segregated education. Operating a two-tier system of special schools and mainstream schools can be an extremely expensive model, with little evidence of extra benefits for the extra costs (Crowther *et al.*, 1998). However, there is understandable cynicism amongst parents and others who view Government moves towards inclusive schools as mechanisms for saving money. Stories of disabled pupils being placed in mainstream provision without adequate resources to support their learning are commonplace. This can lead to a kind of internal exclusion. You can use your developing understanding of concepts of inclusive education to evaluate whether, in your view, this 'inclusion on the cheap' is really inclusive education at all. In our view, such poorly resourced projects undermine genuine advocates of inclusive education who aspire to nothing of this kind.

## A tentative commitment

Some advocates of inclusive education are far more tentative about inclusion than others. They (e.g. Garner and Gains, 2000) talk about 'responsible inclusion' as the only acceptable inclusion, that is, when all the resources are in place and special practices are transferred to the new context. As Alan Dyson (2001) observes, however, the inclusion they describe is actually 'something less like inclusion and more like "old-fashioned" integration' (p. 27). The concept of 'responsible inclusion' carries with it an implication that other inclusion is irresponsible. According to your own individual perspective, you might view 'responsible inclusion', with all its caveats, as just another vision of inclusive education, or, alternatively, as part of a backlash against inclusion, in which practical tensions and difficulties undermine the ideal altogether. For some writers (such as John Wilson, 1999) the dangers inherent in inclusive education for balancing all needs are seen as largely insurmountable.

## A need for evidence?

Some academics who adopt a tentative position call for evidence that inclusive education works before embarking on this project. Seamus Hegarty (1993) and Peter Farrell (1997) have sought to weigh up the balance of evidence from a range of studies. But because it is so hard to accurately match groups or compare outcomes, there are always numerous caveats to any conclusions that can be drawn from the research. This means that the search for an evidence base for moving to inclusion is seen by many as meaningless. Gary Thomas (1997) takes issue with the desire for evidence and argues that educational inclusion is part of a bigger social inclusion agenda and therefore not a matter for judgement based on narrow and often inadequate educational research. Similarly, Peter Mittler (2000a) maintains that the time for evidence is past, as the human rights agenda has made it irrelevant.

## A need for compromise?

Some academics, such as Garry Hornby and Roger Kidd, look for compromises. They focus on schooling as preparation for adulthood and argue that an outcome of high social inclusion in adult life may justify less than full inclusion at school; indeed, that special schools might be better at achieving this outcome. This is the gradualist, step-by-step approach to reaching a goal that Peter Mittler (2000b) has come to question. He compares it to the 'Direct Placement Model' in which you ask 'Where do you want this person to finish?' (p. 105). If the answer is 'fully included in society' then you start with a fully inclusive placement with high levels of support – and reduce that support as and when you can. A better question, of course, would be 'Where does this person want to finish?' We might reasonably ask how exclusion at school can possibly prepare children and young people for active, democratic participation in adult life. Moreover, childhood is not a rehearsal for life, it is life, and how can we justify separating out children for less humane treatment than we would tolerate for adults?

The vision of inclusive education held by Hornby and Kidd (2001) involves the specialized curricula and specialist teachers of special schools moved wholesale into mainstream contexts. Mel Ainscow (1997), in contrast, argues that rather than 'transplant special education thinking' (p. 3) we must look to the best practice of ordinary teachers as a starting point. Susan Hart (1996) has similarly made a convincing case that it is better for ordinary teachers to have self-belief about 'their own power to take positive action in response to concerns about children's learning' (p. x) than to be restrained by special education thinking. The former can avoid 'individualizing the "problem", or disconnecting it' from the context in which it arises (p. x).

## Inclusive education as idealistic

Whilst the recommendations of Ainscow, Hart and others are very practical, inclusive education does come under attack for being idealistic. Those who stress the pragmatic difficulties of inclusion, such as Colin Low (1997), often position themselves in opposition to idealism and ideology. Paul Croll and Diana Moses (2000, p. 1) stress that, while being supportive of inclusion, they see 'meeting children's individual needs' as more important than 'ideological commitment to inclusionist ideals'. The assumption here is that the two are mutually exclusive, and we question this. Croll and Moses have considerable reservations about the capacity of mainstream schools' resources and funding to meet the needs of all children. Thus, they suggest that special schools still have a role to play with regard to children with severe learning difficulties and emotional and behavioural difficulties. From a rights perspective this is, of course, a nonsense, but this is not the position that Croll and Moses are arguing from.

Peter Farrell (2001, p. 7) describes 'arguments in favour of inclusion based solely on human rights' as 'logically and conceptually naïve' because they focus on rights to inclusive education above rights to good education or preferred education. From this position, inclusive education is based too much on emotion and values rather than rational argument or logic. Gary Thomas and Andrew Loxley (2001), however, note that those who attempt to negate inclusive education as irrational ideology fail to recognize that they too are taking an ideological stance; they are talking from a values position but fail to see this.

A problem with attacking idealism is that realists often have low expectations. As Peter Mittler reflects:

> If someone had said to me, when I was training as a clinical psychologist, the day will come before you retire when people with Down syndrome will get GCSEs, or the day will come when you will be invited by people with Down syndrome to their meeting which they will chair and run, I would have thought they were being 'unrealistic'. But in fact that is precisely what has happened.
>
> *(Mittler, 2000b, p. 105)*

It is our view that the dichotomy between ideals and reality is a false and unhelpful one. An ideological position does not have to be unrealistic. When the Committee chaired by John Tomlinson called for widening participation and more inclusive learning in the further education sector, they were clear about their realism:

> Everything we propose is within the grasp of the system if we all want it enough, because its full growth or its seeds are already present somewhere: we are not recommending an idealistic dream, but the reality of extending widely the high quality which already exists in pockets, locked in the minds and actions of the few who must become the many.
>
> *(Tomlinson, 1996, p. 11)*

 ## Activity 6.6   Insurmountable challenges?

The statements below summarize some of the practical challenges of inclusive education that some writers describe as almost insurmountable. Do you find this realistic? Does failure to address these challenges represent an opting out of responsibility? Make a note of the challenges in your learning journal and add to them if you wish. Then note some ways in which schools might address the problems. As you come across examples of good practice in the course materials you can add to this. Are the solutions a matter of tinkering with existing practice or changing it more radically? Working on this exercise will help you to collate examples that you might use in your assignments.

There are not enough resources in ordinary schools to cope with the diverse needs of all pupils.

There is not enough professional expertise in ordinary schools to cope with the diverse needs of all pupils.

Teachers cannot make lessons challenging for pupils with a wide range of abilities.

Ordinary classroom experiences cannot be made meaningful for pupils who have profound intellectual impairment.

Teachers cannot cope with the stress that great diversity brings.

Ordinary schools cannot prepare pupils for independent living.

## Summary

In this section we have looked at the ways in which concerns with pragmatism shape some concepts of inclusive education. This may inform the debate on how inclusion might be achieved or it may hold back action in a desire to see proof or perfect conditions in place prior to making real changes. It might be helpful to consider whose problems are being put at the forefront when inclusion is cast as problematic. Invariably integration was and inclusion may be seen as problematic *for professionals*, but it is segregation that is problematic *for disabled and other oppressed pupils*.

# 6 The moral imperative for inclusion

These experiences made me angry, and that anger made me into a rebel ... Social justice is therefore something that drives me. It's a very strong motivator. I can't bear to see unfairness, and I am driven to speak out.

*(Corker, 2000, p. 74)*

Inclusive education is part of a human rights approach to social relations and conditions. The intentions and values

involved relate to a vision of the whole society of which
education is a part. Issues of social justice, equity and
choice are central to the demands for inclusive education.

*(Barton, Reader 1, Chapter 6, p. 59)*

Principles are the key. Research can provide only a crude
pointer to the success or appropriateness of inclusion.
Ultimately, whether or not desegregation proceeds and
mainstream schools become more inclusive will hinge on
society's values and its attitudes. If inclusion succeeds in
displacing special segregated education it will have done
so because society considers that it is right to do so.

*(Thomas, 1997, p. 104)*

As these quotations illustrate, we end this unit with visions of inclusive
education based on a moral stance or disability/human rights
perspective. From this perspective inclusive education is not just about
education, but about social inclusion and a fundamental issue of
human rights. Inclusion is seen as 'the logical development of a more
tolerant and accepting society, an extension of the basic human right
for all people to participate in that society regardless of any difference
or disability' (Rouse and Florian, 1997, p. 323). The moral imperative
for inclusion is clearly articulated in the Salamanca Statement (see
Unit 2).

## Inclusion as a political struggle

When visions of inclusive education are informed by a disability
rights perspective they are often accompanied by a highly critical
stance on special education. Despite its benign face, special education
is seen or experienced as a means of oppression of those pupils caught
up in it. Inclusion from this perspective becomes a political struggle
(Vlachou, 1997) against systems that seek to maintain and rationalize
the marginalization of those they claim to help. This vision of the
journey to inclusion is less a rocky pathway and more a battleground:
it is a direct fight to remove injustices (Barton, 1997).

The Direct Action Network (DAN), a civil rights organization of
disabled people and their supporters, is committed to direct action to
achieve their goals. Amongst disability activists are disabled adults,
who, describing themselves as special school survivors, demand an
end to segregated education. The DAN charter outlines the demands
being raised by the disability movement. In terms of education these
include:

- Close segregated educational facilities

- An end to statementing

- Full and equal access to all educational institutions

- Control over the equipment and resources necessary to ensure equal access to education

- Equal access to the full curriculum

- Employment of disabled staff throughout the education system.

*(DAN, 2002)*

Like DAN, the Centre for Studies in Inclusive Education (CSIE), is committed to campaigning for inclusive education as a human rights issue. CSIE's 'ten reasons for inclusion' are based on inclusive education being a human right, being good education and making good social sense. The human rights focus stresses that all children have the right to learn together and that children should not be devalued or discriminated against by being excluded or sent away because of their impairment or learning difficulty.

**Table 6.1   CSIE's ten reasons for inclusion.**

| | | |
|---|---|---|
| HUMAN RIGHTS | 1 | All children have the right to learn together |
| | 2 | Children should not be devalued or discriminated against by being excluded or sent away because of their disability or learning difficulty. |
| | 3 | Disabled adults, describing themselves as special school survivors, are demanding an end to segregation. |
| | 4 | There are no legitimate reasons to separate children for their education. Children belong together – with advantages and benefits for everyone. They do not need to be protected from each other. |
| GOOD EDUCATION | 5 | Research shows children do better, academically and socially, in inclusive settings. |
| | 6 | There is no teaching or care in a segregated school which cannot take place in an ordinary school. |
| | 7 | Given commitment and support, inclusive education is a more efficient use of educational resources. |
| SOCIAL SENSE | 8 | Segregation teaches children to be fearful, ignorant and breeds prejudice. |
| | 9 | All children need an education that will help them develop relationships and prepare them for life in the mainstream. |
| | 10 | Only inclusion has the potential to reduce fear and to build friendship, respect and understanding. |

*(Source: CSIE, 2002)*

##  Activity 6.7    Demands and reasons

Think about how you respond to DAN's charter and CSIE's points. Can you identify arguments to defend or attack DAN's demands?

Your arguments might be based, for example, on your own experience of what it feels like to be excluded, or research you have come across about the academic outcomes for pupils in inclusive placements.

## An inclusive school ethos

Also belonging to a cluster of views within a human rights perspective is the concept of inclusion as an extension of the comprehensive ideal. The importance of social mixing is emphasized in this perspective as something from which everyone benefits, because 'children belong together' (CSIE, 2002). The notion underlying this is that we all learn from exposure to difference; in inclusive education all children become more compassionate and gain a better sense of community (Dorries and Haller, Reader 1, Chapter 23).

Some texts, including the *Index for Inclusion* (Booth *et al.*, 2000) focus on the particular school ethos or culture in inclusive education. We include this perspective here as it is based on concerns with the values that are communicated and taught in schools. In inclusive school cultures it is the learner who drives the educational experience and not the teacher or the curriculum (Carrington, 1999). Teachers listen rather than just talk and the concern with listening to learners links inclusive education with self-advocacy and with democracy.

Dorothy Lipsky and Alan Gartner (1999) see inclusive education and democracy as more than just linked. They argue that inclusive education is more than a characteristic of a democratic society – it is essential to it. From this standpoint, whatever a learner's difference, enjoying active participation in a school community is a matter of being a full member of society and a question of citizenship.

Human rights perspectives on inclusive education very importantly celebrate rather than merely tolerate difference. Len Barton sums this up when he states that 'inclusive education is about responding to diversity; it is about listening to unfamiliar voices, being open, empowering all members and about celebrating "difference" in dignified ways' (1997, p. 233). Difference such as an impairment is regarded as a prompt to change and enhance educational practice, and 'to question unfounded generalizations, prejudice and discrimination' (p. 235).

The Alliance for Inclusive Education (2002) build their case for
inclusion on eight principles:

- A person's worth is independent of their abilities or achievements
- Every human being is able to feel and think
- Every human being has a right to communicate and be heard
- All human beings need each other
- Real education can only happen in the context of real relationships
- All people need support and friendship from people of their own age
- Progress for all learners is achieved by building on things people can do rather than what they can't
- Diversity brings strength to all living systems.

## Activity 6.8    The politics

Now read Chapter 6, 'The politics of education for all' by Len
Barton, in Reader 1. As you read, make a note of the key
arguments.

Now imagine you are a teacher adopting the position that a
human rights inclusionist stance like this one is too idealist. Jot
down arguments you might present to Len Barton and the
responses he might in turn make to you.

This exercise will help you to rehearse the skills you will need in
TMA 02.

## Summary

Concepts of inclusive education are often intricately entwined with
concepts of social justice, human rights and democracy. As Peter
Mittler (2000a) makes clear, when one adopts the position that
inclusive education is a moral imperative then the issue no longer
becomes whether or not inclusive education is right but how it can
best be achieved.

# 7 Conclusion

In this unit you will have seen that we cannot just talk about what inclusive education *is,* without recognizing that it is different things to different people, in different contexts and at different moments in time. A central purpose of this course is that it will enable you as students to have a different perspective on what inclusive education is at the end of studying it than the one you had at the beginning. You might like to take stock on whether this is happening. Your own perspective is likely to become more complex, but as your understanding deepens, you should be able to identify what the key elements are for you.

The final exercise in this unit is intended to help you to digest and make sense of the material you have read.

 ## Activity 6.9   Your views

### Part 1

Read through the list of definitions of inclusion below. Use these to help you to recap on the theoretical input from the unit. Then sort the definitions into those that are closest to and those that are farthest from your own personal views.

---

### Definitions of inclusion

Being with one another ... how we deal with diversity, how we deal with difference (Forest and Pearpoint, 1992)

Inclusive schools are diverse problem-solving organizations with a common mission that emphasizes learning for all students (Rouse and Florian, 1996)

Being a full member of an age-appropriate class in your local school doing the same lessons as the other pupils and it mattering if you are not there. Plus you have friends who spend time with you outside of school (Hall, 1996)

A set of principles which ensures that the student with a disability is viewed as a valued and needed member of the school community in every respect (Uditsky, 1993)

Inclusion can be understood as a move towards extending the scope of 'ordinary' schools so they can include a greater diversity of children (Clark *et al.,* 1995)

---

Inclusive schools deliver a curriculum to students through organisational arrangements that are different from those used in schools that exclude some students from their regular classrooms (Ballard, 1995)

Increasing participation and decreasing exclusion from mainstream social settings (Potts, 1997)

Inclusion describes the process by which a school attempts to respond to all pupils as individuals by reconsidering its curricula organisation and provision (Sebba, 1996)

An inclusive school is one which is accepting of all children (Thomas, 1997)

*(Florian, 1998, p. 16)*

## Part 2

Use all of these definitions and phrases, and any other particularly poignant ones that you may have highlighted as you read through the unit, to complete a grid like the one below. This will enable you to think about inclusive education in terms of a range of important dimensions. You may find less to say about the curriculum and teaching and learning dimensions at this stage, but you may find it useful revision to add more after you have read Units 7, 8 and 13.

| Dimensions of inclusion | |
|---|---|
| Values/ethical dimension | |
| Organizational dimension | |
| Curricular dimension | |
| Teaching and learning dimension | |

 A grid we have started can be found in Appendix 2 (p. 90).

You may be tempted to think that, because inclusive education is such a buzzword of our time, it is a phase that will pass. However, even if government interest fades, inclusion as a political struggle for disabled people will remain. We tend to support Lani Florian's comment that:

> Although this [inclusive education] means different things in different places there is a universality to the underlying human rights philosophy of inclusion which suggests that the concept is destined to persist rather than represent the latest educational fad or bandwagon.
>
> *(Florian, 1998, p. 13)*

We can also see that we are at the beginning of what is a long-term project in inclusive education. Establishing the human right to inclusion has created a foundation on which inclusive practice is beginning to be built. When you read the following units exploring the perspectives on inclusive education of pupils, parents and professionals, you might like to reflect on what they say should be happening to build on this foundation. It seems to us that one of the challenges is to establish a framework of *different but equal* in relation to educational experiences as well as learners. By this we do not mean separate and equal. Instead we are saying that celebrating the diverse learners participating in inclusive education does not mean requiring all eight year olds, for example, to follow the same curriculum in the same way at the same time. Nor does it mean differentiating them into the hierarchical tiers associated with the tripartite system, the special school system, setting and streaming, or specialist schools. The alternative is horizontal diversity with rich and varied educational experiences offered in ways that do not categorize learners and fence them in to pre-specified pathways. This vision of inclusive education is both viable and in some ways revolutionary; it does more than tinker with changes to the current system and ethos.

What does your vision of inclusive education look like? To make sense of this unit you need to be able to critique and evaluate the perspectives you have been introduced to, to inform your own position. You do not, however, have to over-simplify ideas that are by their very nature complex. In this unit we have shown that inclusive education as a construct is fluid and contentious. Inclusion is socially constructed and socially created by people who have passionate ideas about it. As Rosenthal argues, vital to any journey towards inclusive education is that we listen to each other's diverse voices:

> To address discrimination and move towards more fully promoting the inclusion agenda, we have to provide regular meaningful dialogues ... **and** we have to individually examine and adjust our own less-social perceptions, values and actions. All of us need to experience and hear each other's points of view, and the differences between us have to be acknowledged and explored, rather than ignored and denied.
>
> *(Rosenthal, 2001, p. 385)*

# References

Ainscow, M. (1994) *Special Needs in the Classroom: a teacher education guide*, London, Jessica Kingsley/UNESCO.

Ainscow, M. (1997) 'Towards inclusive schooling', *British Journal of Special Education*, **24**(1), pp. 3–6.

Ainscow, M. (2000) 'Profile' in Clough, P. and Corbett, J. (eds) *Theories of Inclusive Education: a students' guide*, London, Paul Chapman.

Aird, R. (2001) *The Education and Care of Children with Severe, Profound and Multiple Learning Difficulties*, London, David Fulton.

Allan, J. (1999) *Actively Seeking Inclusion: pupils with special needs in mainstream schools*, London, Falmer Press.

Allan, J. (2000) 'Reflection: inconclusive education? Towards settled uncertainty' in Clough, P. and Corbett, J. (eds) *Theories of Inclusive Education: a students' guide*, London, Paul Chapman.

Alliance for Inclusive Education (2001) *Inclusion Now*, Spring 2001.

Alliance for Inclusive Education (2002) http://www.allfie.org.uk/pages/principles [accessed 27 January 2003].

Ball, S. J. (1994) *Education Reform: a critical and post-structural approach*, Open University Press, Buckingham.

Ballard, K. (1995) 'Inclusion, paradigms, power and participation' in Clark, C., Dyson, A. and Millward, A. (eds) *Towards Inclusive Schools?* London, David Fulton.

Barton, L. (1997) 'Inclusive education: romantic, subversive or realistic?', *International Journal of Inclusive Education*, **1**(3), pp. 231–42.

Barton, L. (1998) *The Politics of Special Educational Needs,* Lewes, London, Falmer Press.

Bines, H. (2001) 'A longer road to inclusion', *Support for Learning*, **16**(2), pp. 92–3.

Blamires, M. (1999) 'Universal design for learning: re-establishing differentiation as part of the inclusion agenda?', *Support for Learning*, **14**(4), pp. 158–63.

Booth, T. (1995) 'Mapping inclusion and exclusion: concepts for all?' in Clark, C., Dyson, A. and Millward, A. (eds) *Towards Inclusive Schools?*, London, David Fulton.

Booth, T. (1996) 'Stories of exclusion: natural and unnatural selection' in Blythe, E. and Milner, J. (eds) *Exclusion from School: inter-professional issues for policy and practice*, London, Routledge.

Booth, T., Ainscow, M., Black-Hawkins, K., Vaughan, M. and Shaw, L. (2000) *Index for Inclusion: developing learning and participation in schools*, Bristol, CSIE.

Carrington, S. (1999) 'Inclusion needs a different school culture', *Journal of Inclusive Education*, **1**(1), pp. 55–64.

Clark, C., Dyson, A. and Millward, A. (1995) *Towards Inclusive Schools?* London, David Fulton.

Clough, P. (2000) 'Routes to inclusion' in Clough, P. and Corbett, J. (eds) *Theories of Inclusive Education: a students' guide*, London, Paul Chapman

Corbett, J. (1997) 'Include/exclude: redefining the boundaries', *International Journal of Inclusive Education*, 1(1), pp. 55–64.

Corbett, J. (1999) 'Inclusive education and school culture', *International Journal of Inclusive Education*, 3(1), pp. 53–61.

Corker, M. (2000) 'Profile' in Clough, P. and Corbett, J. (eds) *Theories of Inclusive Education: a students' guide*, London, Paul Chapman.

Croll, P. and Moses, D. (1998) 'Pragmatism, ideology and educational change: the case of special educational needs', *British Journal of Educational Studies*, 46(1), pp. 11–25.

Croll, P. and Moses, D. (2000) 'Ideologies and utopias: education professionals' views of inclusion', *European Journal of Special Needs Education*, 15(1), pp. 1–12.

Crowther, D., Dyson, A. and Millward, A. (1998) *Costs and Outcomes for Pupils with Moderate Learning Difficulties in Special and Mainstream Schools*, Research Report RR89, London, DfEE.

CSIE (Centre for Studies in Inclusive Education) (2002) http://www.CSIE.org.uk [accessed 27 January 2003].

CSIE (Centre for Studies in Inclusive Education) (2003) http://inclusion.uwe.ac.uk/csie/indexlaunch.htm [accessed 26 October 2003].

DAN (Direct Action Network) (2002) http://dspace.dial.pipex.com/town/square/de95/c_dancht.htm#charter [accessed 27 January 2003].

Dyson, A. (2001) 'Special needs in the twenty-first century: where we've been and where we're going', *British Journal of Special Education*, 28(1), pp. 24–9.

Farrell, P. (1997) 'The integration of children with severe learning difficulties: a review of the recent literature', *Journal of Applied Research in Intellectual Disabilities*, 10(1), pp. 1–14.

Farrell, P. (2001) 'Special education in the last twenty years: have things really got better?', *British Journal of Special Education*, 28(1), pp. 3–9.

Finkelstein, V. (1996) 'We want to remodel the world', Editorial, *DAIL Magazine*, 4 October 1996.

Florian, L., Rose, R. and Tilstone, C. (1998) 'Pragmatism not dogmatism: promoting more inclusive practice' in Tilstone, C., Florian, L. and Rose, R. (eds) *Promoting Inclusive Practice*, London, Routledge.

Florian, L. (1998) 'Inclusive practice: what, why and how?' in Tilstone, C., Florian, L. and Rose, R. (eds) *Promoting Inclusive Practice*, London, Routledge.

Forest, M. and Pearpoint, J. (1992) 'Putting all kids on the MAP', *Educational Leadership*, **50**(2), pp. 26–31.

Garner, P. and Gains, C. (2000) 'The debate that never happened!', *Special!*, Autumn, pp. 8–11.

Germon, P. (1999) 'Activists and academics: part of the same or a world apart?' in Shakespeare, T. (ed.) *The Disability Reader: social science perspectives*, London, Cassell.

Hall, J. (1996) 'Integration, inclusion, – what does it all mean?' in Coupe O'Kane, J. and Goldbart, J. (eds) *Whose Choice? Contentious issues for those working with people with learning difficulties*, London, David Fulton.

Hart, S. (1996) *Beyond Special Needs: enhancing children's learning through innovative thinking*, London, Paul Chapman.

Hegarty, S. (1993) 'Reviewing the literature on integration', *European Journal of Special Needs Education*, **8**(3), pp. 194–200.

Hornby, G. and Kidd, R. (2001) 'Transfer from special to mainstream – ten years later', *British Journal of Special Education*, **28**(1), pp. 10–17.

Inclusion Network Marsha Forest Centre (2003) http://www.inclusion.com.

Lewis, A. (1995) *Primary Special Needs and the National Curriculum* (second edition), London, Routledge.

Lipsky, D. K. and Gartner, A. (1999) 'Inclusive education: a requirement of a democratic society' in Daniels, H. and Garner, P. (eds) *Inclusive Education: supporting inclusion in education systems*, London, Kogan Page.

Low, C. (1997) 'Is inclusivism possible?', *European Journal of Special Needs Education*, **12**(1), pp. 71–9.

Mittler, P. (2000a) *Working Towards Inclusive Education: social contexts*, London, David Fulton.

Mittler, P. (2000b) 'Profile' in Clough, P. and Corbett, J. (eds) *Theories of Inclusive Education: a students' guide*, London, Paul Chapman.

Nind, M. (2002) 'Some neglected common ground? Early childhood education and special needs education', *Westminster Studies in Education*, **25**(1), pp. 77–90.

Ofsted (2002) http://www.ofsted.gov.uk, p. 4 [accessed 8 March 2002].

Oliver, M. (1996) *The Politics of Disablement*, Basingstoke, MacMillan.

Oliver, M. (2000a) 'Profile' in Clough, P. and Corbett, J. (eds) *Theories of Inclusive Education: a students' guide*, London, Paul Chapman.

Oliver, M. (2000b) 'Decoupling education policy from the economy in late capitalist societies: some implications for special education', keynote address at ISEC 2000, 'Including the Excluded', Manchester, July.

Potts, P. (1997) 'Developing a collaborative approach to the study of inclusive education in more than one country', paper presented to the European Conference on Educational Research, Frankfurt am Main, September.

Rosenthal, H. (2001) 'Working towards inclusion: "I am another other"', *Educational Psychology in Practice,* **17**(4), pp. 385–92.

Rouse, M. and Florian, L. (1996) 'Effective inclusive schools: a study in two countries', *Cambridge Journal of Education,* **26**(1), pp. 71–85.

Rouse, M. and Florian, L. (1997) 'Inclusive education in the market place', *International Journal of Inclusive Education,* **1**(4), 323–36.

Sebba, J. (1996) *Developing Inclusive Schools,* Cambridge, University of Cambridge Institute of Education.

Sebba, J. and Ainscow, M. (1996) 'International developments in inclusive schooling: mapping the issues', *Cambridge Journal of Education,* **26**(1), pp. 5–18.

Sebba, J. and Sachdev, D. (1997) *What Works in Inclusive Education,* London, Barnardos.

Slee, R. (1999) 'Policies and practices? Inclusive education and its effects on schooling' in Daniels, H. and Garner, P. (eds) *Inclusive Education: supporting inclusion in education systems,* London, Kogan Page.

Swann, W. (1992) 'Hardening the hierarchies: the national curriculum as a system of classification' in Booth, T., Swann, W., Masterton, M. and Potts, P. (eds) *Curricula for Diversity in Education,* London, Routledge/The Open University.

Thomas, G. (1997) 'Inclusive schools for an inclusive society', *British Journal of Special Education,* **24**(3), pp. 103–7.

Thomas, G. and Loxley, A. (2001) *Deconstructing Special Education and Constructing Inclusion,* Buckingham, Open University Press.

Thomas, G., Walker, D. and Webb, J. (1998) *The Making of the Inclusive School,* London, Routledge.

Thomas, G. and Loxley, A. (2001) *Deconstructing Special Education and Constructing Inclusion,* Buckingham, Open University Press.

Tomlinson, J. (1996) *Inclusive Learning: principles and recommendations. A summary of the findings of the Learning Difficulties and/or Disabilities Committee,* London, Further Education Funding Council.

Uditsky, B. (1993) 'From integration to inclusion: the Canadian experience' in Slee, R. (ed.) *Is There a Desk with My Name on It? The politics of integration,* London, Falmer Press.

Vlachou, A. D. (1997) *Struggles for Inclusive Education,* Buckingham, Open University Press.

Ware, J. (1997) 'Implementing the 1988 Education Reform Act with pupils with PMLDs' in Ware, J. (ed.) *Educating Children with Profound and Multiple Learning Difficulties,* London, David Fulton.

Wilson, J. (1999) 'Some conceptual difficulties about inclusion', *Support for Learning*, **14**(3), pp. 110–12.

# Appendix 1
# Indicators from the *Index for Inclusion*

**DIMENSION A**   **Creating inclusive CULTURES**

*A.1*   *Building community*

INDICATOR

A.1.1   Everyone is made to feel welcome.

A.1.2   Students help each other.

A.1.3   Staff collaborate with each other.

A.1.4   Staff and students treat one another with respect.

A.1.5   There is a partnership between staff and parents/carers.

A.1.6   Staff and governors work well together.

A.1.7   All local communities are involved in the school.

*A.2*   *Establishing inclusive values*

INDICATOR

A.2.1
     There are high expectations for all students.

A.2.2   Staff, governors, students and parents/carers share a philosophy of inclusion.

A.2.3   Students are equally valued.

A.2.4   Staff and students treat one another as human beings as well as occupants of a 'role'.

A.2.5   Staff seek to remove barriers to learning and participation in all aspects of the school.

A.2.6   The school strives to minimise discriminatory practices.

### DIMENSION B   Producing inclusive POLICIES

*B.1*   *Developing the school for all*

INDICATOR

B.1.1   Staff appointments and promotions are fair.

B.1.2   All new staff are helped to settle into the school.

B.1.3   The school seeks to admit all students from its locality.

B.1.4   The school makes its buildings physically accessible to all people.

B.1.5   All new students are helped to settle into the school.

B.1.6   The school arranges teaching groups so that all students are valued.

*B.2*   *Organising support for diversity*

INDICATOR

B.2.1   All forms of support are co-ordinated.

B.2.2   Staff development activities help staff to respond to student diversity.

B.2.3   'Special educational needs' policies are inclusion policies.

B.2.4   The Special Educational Needs Code of Practice is used to reduce the barriers to learning and participation of all students.

B.2.5   Support for those learning English as an additional language is co-ordinated with learning support.

B.2.6   Pastoral and behaviour support policies are linked to curriculum development and learning support policies.

B.2.7   Pressures for disciplinary exclusion are decreased.

B.2.8   Barriers to attendance are reduced.

B.2.9   Bullying is minimised.

## DIMENSION C   Evolving inclusive PRACTICES

| C.1 | *Orchestrating learning* |
|---|---|

INDICATOR

| C.1.1 | Teaching is planned with the learning of all students in mind. |
|---|---|
| C.1.2 | Lessons encourage the participation of all students. |
| C.1.3 | Lessons develop an understanding of difference. |
| C.1.4 | Students are actively involved in their own learning. |
| C.1.5 | Students learn collaboratively. |
| C.1.6 | Assessment contributes to the achievements of all students. |
| C.1.7 | Classroom discipline is based on mutual respect. |
| C.1.8 | Teachers plan, teach and review in partnership. |
| C.1.9 | Teachers are concerned to support the learning and participation of all students. |
| C.1.10 | Teaching assistants support the learning and participation of all students. |
| C.1.11 | Homework contributes to the learning of all. |
| C.1.12 | All students take part in activities outside the classroom. |

| C.2 | *Mobilising resources* |
|---|---|

INDICATOR

| C.2.1 | Student difference is used as a resource for teaching and learning. |
|---|---|
| C.2.2 | Staff expertise is fully utilised. |
| C.2.3 | Staff develop resources to support learning and participation. |
| C.2.4 | Community resources are known and drawn upon. |
| C.2.5 | School resources are distributed fairly so that they support inclusion. |

*(CSIE, 2003, http://inclusion/uwe.ac.uk/csie/indexlaunch.htm)*

# Appendix 2
# Dimensions of inclusion

| Dimensions of inclusion | |
|---|---|
| Values/ethical dimension | Diversity is ordinary and valued<br>All children are welcome in schools<br>Separate is not equal<br>Participation is a democratic right |
| Organizational dimension | Children should learn together in their local school<br>School arrangements should fit around learners rather than learners fitting into school arrangements |
| Curricular dimension | Diverse children share the same lessons |
| Teaching and learning dimension | Teaching styles need to suit diverse learners, rather than learners having to cope with teachers' preferred teaching styles |

# UNIT 7 Seen but not heard?

*Prepared for the course team by Kieron Sheehy and Katy Simmons*

## Contents

# 1   Introduction

In this unit we look at inclusive education from the perspective of the groups who are particularly affected by the issues raised by this course – children and parents who are the users of services. But how far have their experiences been considered as these services have developed? In this unit we will look at what children and parents think and feel, at how they are making their voices heard and at the impact that their experiences have had on the responses of governments and providers of services. One of the keynotes of inclusive practice, in the view of the authors of this course, is that diverse voices are acknowledged and valued.

The first part of the unit sets a context for listening to these diverse voices. We move from some ideas about people being more than 'single categories' and present some challenging thoughts about how we might avoid 'pigeonholing', and consequently ignoring, other people's views. Our arguments for including such diverse views are based on personal, educational and human rights perspectives.

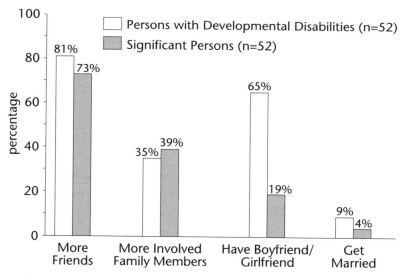

Figure 7.1   *A comparison of requests for new relationships from people with learning difficulties and those who were 'significant people' in their lives (Froese et al., 1999, p. 836).*

In exploring these themes in this unit we are aware of the relationship between the construction of people's identities and how they interact with the education system. We look at parents and children together because, generally speaking, both groups of people might be seen as 'users' of services. We are aware, though, that their interests are not always the same. For example, in a study conducted in the USA, Paul

Froese and colleagues (1999) interviewed people with a 'developmental disability' and people who were significant in their lives. The latter group were mostly parents. They found a contrast in opinions across a range of questions.

You will see from the graphs in Figure 7.1 that the views of the two groups of people varied considerably, especially when they were asked about personal relationships.

Some writers, for example Simone Aspis (2001), have seen parents as contributing to the oppression that young disabled people can experience. Parents have more legal rights than their children, as well as better-developed advocacy systems; some writers would argue that parents' voices have been unduly powerful. Although we have grouped the interests of parents and children together for the purposes of this unit, we acknowledge these imbalances of power and bear them in mind. The first activity is an opportunity to start thinking about your own perspective on these imbalances.

## Activity 7.1   Conflicts of interest

The data in Figure 7.1 illustrated the differing perspectives of people with 'development disability' and their parents over the issue of relationships in their lives. Can you think of any issues or situations over which parents and children might hold differing or conflicting views? These could be issues related to social, educational, or domestic spheres. You may find stories and themes that prompt your ideas in television programmes, radio documentary and drama, films, music or your own daily life.

In your learning journal, make a note of your examples. Can you identify how their priorities related to these might differ?

Consider whether particular groups of young people, such as young disabled people or children with learning difficulties, would be likely to have different experiences and views on the situations and issues you identify.

We begin the unit by considering the views of pupils and reflections on school experiences. These insights provide a context in which to consider Charlotte Carter and Audrey Osler's model for developing an inclusive ethos within schools. This model explicitly includes and acknowledges the perspectives of members of the school community.

## Learning outcomes

By end of this unit you will:

- have developed an understanding of a context in which listening to the perspectives of others is important in developing inclusive education;

- understand how different models of special and inclusive education have shaped the experiences of parents;

- have gained insights into the varying perspectives of parents and children;

- have reflected on how children's and parents' perspectives fit into your developing model of good practice and how they relate to your own perspectives.

## Resources for this unit

In tackling the activities in this unit you will need to draw on a variety of resources.

Activity 7.1 asks you to think about parents' and children's viewpoints. You may need to draw on the media to prompt your ideas: television programmes, radio documentary and drama, films, music or your own daily life.

Activity 7.4 involves observing children in their interactions with adults and the adult world. You will need to create some opportunities to make observations either in daily life or through the media.

Activity 7.5 requires you to discuss a concept from the course with a friend, so you will need to identify a peer or colleague who you would like to do this with and plan some time together to devote to this.

Activity 7.7 for this you will need to do some research on groups which campaign on behalf of children, which may involve looking on the internet or contacting your local library.

As part of your study for this unit you will be asked to read the following chapters from the readers:

For Activity 7.2:

- Chapter 4, 'The stairs don't go anywhere' by Michael F. Giangreco, in Reader 1.

For Activity 7.6:

- Chapter 3, 'Child and parent relationships with teachers in schools responsible for the education of children with serious medical conditions' by Claire Norris and Alison Closs, in Reader 2.

For Activity 7.8:

- Chapter 23, 'The news of inclusive education: a narrative analysis' by Bruce Dorries and Beth Haller, in Reader 1.

## Experiences of inclusion and exclusion

We have examined, in earlier units, the ways in which language can be used to construct people and their lives in certain ways. Clearly a person's sense of identity (who they think they are, what they should do and the potential futures that they work towards) is powerfully affected by these constructions. For example, in the mental handicap 'hospitals' of the 1950s and 1960s – even continuing into the 1970s in some cases – adult 'patients' were identified as 'boys' and 'girls' and segregated. This use of language constructed these people as ill and childlike and validated enforced segregation and the denial of their right to adult relationships (Atkinson, Jackson and Walmsley, 1997).

Our identities are constructed historically and culturally. For example, the writers of this unit might be seen as 'special education professionals' in that we are paid to write the unit. But we both have experience of disability through our disabled parents and in that sense have been users of services, rather than providers, for many years. As you read through this unit consider how the identities of the people whose voices are presented are influenced by the social world of which they are a part and the language that is used within that social world. We have already seen cases of struggle where people are fighting to construct their own identity in the world, for example disability activists in Unit 4 or special school 'survivors' in Unit 2. In situations such as these the formation of a strong group identity is needed as part of the process of empowerment and change, so that individuals begin to see themselves not as isolated victims, but as part of a wider group of people whose experiences have much in common. To see people entirely in terms of a single categorization denies the complex nature of people and their lives: parents can be disabled people too; teachers can be parents; children may move in and out of categories of 'special need' as defined by school; and all of us have a gender, an ethnicity and a sexuality. A first step in 'going beyond the label' is to listen to what a person is saying about different aspects of his or her life.

## Activity 7.2   Listening to experience

Now read the following chapter:

- Chapter 4, 'The stairs don't go anywhere: a self-advocate's reflections on specialised services and their impact on people with disabilities' by Michael F. Giangreco, in Reader 1.

In this chapter Norman Kunc gives his perspective on a variety of issues that have affected his life. Norman has put himself in a position in which his views can be heard but this was not the case when he was a child.

After reading the chapter, think about whether the points he makes about normalization and functionality are relevant to all children.

Norman puts forward his view that there is a wide diversity in the 'human community' and yet some therapists he encountered wanted to 'normalize' him. Others wanted to make him 'function better' to improve his quality of life. Can you see any parallels between these ideas and the imposition of compulsory curricula and the standards agenda (which we discussed in Unit 2)? Is the goal of these initiatives a form of normalization that includes functionality for children identified as 'having' special educational needs? Is it valid to apply ideas that have arisen from disability rights to the education system overall? In your learning journal write your thoughts on this point. Some of you may agree that this is the case, others may not.

A key point emerging from the interview with Norman Kunc is the importance of listening to the voices of others and relating what they say to an aspect of our own experience. We have seen in Units 5 and 6 how listening to diverse voices (Barton, 1997) is central to many concepts of inclusive education. We suggest here that this listening to others is a sensible route for exploring inclusive education.

## A chance to speak

Our conviction about the significance of the views of others, particularly those of learners themselves, arises from our awareness of the human rights that we possess. You will remember that the United Nations Convention on the Rights of the Child, which we looked at in some detail in Unit 4, is based on principles of participation, inclusion and equity. The UK ratified that Convention in 1994. The 2001 *Special Educational Needs Code of Practice* appeared, on the surface at least, to address this lack of opportunity. The preface asserts that the *Code of Practice* 'places the rights of children with special educational needs at the heart of the process, allowing them to be heard and to take part in decisions about their education' (DfES, 2001a). The *Code of Practice* and the accompanying *SEN Toolkit* (DfES, 2001b) provide advice on pupil participation and enabling pupils to give their views. We observed in Unit 4 that this position has not, however, been reflected in legislation and children and young people lack opportunity, in law, to contribute to decisions about their education.

In addition to the personal and human rights bases for listening to others, there are also educational reasons for considering the learner's perspective. Roger Hancock and Melian Mansfield (2002) list the reasons put forward by various authors in educational literature. Pupils can:

> help professionals better understand the qualities and shortcomings of institutions ...
>
> be action researchers with teachers ...
>
> be helped to feel more involved in school ... and partners in planning ...
>
> be partners in school improvement ...
>
> inform teachers about their teaching ...
>
> give teachers ... and inspectors ... feedback on how school is being experienced;
>
> provide government with feedback on its education policies ...
>
> *(cited in Hancock and Mansfield, 2002, p. 3)*

Hancock and Mansfield go on to suggest that in practice many teachers and schools disregard children's views and perspectives. To support this they cite a study in which only a quarter of 2,272 young people aged seven to seventeen years old thought that teachers took their opinions seriously (Alderson, 1999, cited in Hancock and Mansfield, 2002). Similar concerns have also been raised in relation to the processes of formal assessments of children, for example during the construction of a statement of special educational needs). Professionals are eloquent that the child is the principal client, whose interests are paramount in any assessment. Yet there can be a lack of attention given to the child's voice in the actual assessment (Armstrong, 1995). Derek Armstrong shares one powerful example:

> I've been visited by someone in school called a socialist [*sic*]. I didn't like seeing her because I thought they were going to take me away. I couldn't talk to them and tell them about what I felt. They kept talking and I couldn't get a chance to speak. If I had a chance to speak I would have said I didn't want to go away. I wanted to stay with my parents and family.
>
> *(Child quoted in Armstrong, 1995, p. 91)*

In the consumerist age in which we live, with educational stakeholders and competition given prominence in the arena of public services, it is odd that the direct consumers of education are rarely consulted.

The next section of this unit illustrates the perspectives of learners inside the school system about aspects of education and learning. These examples have been selected as having particular relevance to developing inclusive education.

# 2 What children's perspectives tell us about inclusion

Every child's experience of education is different and this means that inevitably all children will be at different stages of the 'journey' towards inclusion that we are considering in this course. In reflecting children's perspectives it is, therefore, difficult to avoid descriptions of situations that are far from ideal. However, these situations can be seen as steps along the way. This will not, sadly, reduce the impact of unsatisfactory situations on the children themselves. Certainly the education system in the UK has progressed enormously since Mabel Cooper's school days.

> There used to be children, there used to be two wards of children. One for little boys and one for girls. There was no school there, they only let you use your hands by making baskets and doing all that sort of thing. That's all you did. In them days they said you wasn't able to learn so you didn't go to school you went to like a big ward and they had tables. You just went there and made baskets or what-have-you. Because in them days they said you wasn't capable enough to learn to do anything else, so that's what you did.
>
> *(Cooper, 2003)*

Today, after the closure of such institutions, Mabel works for the People First self-advocacy group helping to give a voice to people who have been kept in silence. Within one person's lifetime we have come a long way in what we expect from educational experiences and who we listen to. Society is now beginning to ask people about their experiences and opinions of the services that are designed for them. This may be seen as the start of a more participatory and inclusive approach.

## Why do you come here?

### Children's perceptions of play and learning

An innovative study looked at why children thought they came to their particular schools and centres. Researchers collected the things that children said and analysed the ways in which they said them. The intention behind this was to inform the development of the services the children and their families received (Farrell, Taylor, Tennent and Gahan, 2002). By taking this approach, the children became active and important participants in the work. Building the children's views into the development of their education services was an acknowledgement of their right to participate in the social processes affecting their lives.

> No social organization can hope to be built on the rights
> of its members unless there are mechanisms whereby
> those members may express themselves and wherein
> those expressions are taken seriously. Hearing what
> children say must, therefore, lie at the root of an
> elaboration of children's rights ...
>
> *(Eekelaar, 1992, cited in Farrell et al., 2002)*

Telling stories and playing with narratives about ourselves and experiences is a way in which we build our notions of 'self', who we are and our place in the world (Harrett, 2002).

Iris Keating and her colleagues visited ten primary schools in the north west of England and asked young children about the things that they were doing in their reception classes. One child who had done PE, music and sand in a day commented, 'Well I've not done any work today, I don't know why I came to school' (Keating *et al.*, 2000, p. 443). 'Real work' was identified by children as reading and writing: 'Looking at books. That's not playing. Painting – that's playing. Writing is work' (Keating *et al.*, 2000, p. 443). Moreover, these reception-age children saw play as inferior to work:

*Interviewer:*  You told me that work is important. Is playing important?

*Child:*  No.

*(Keating et al., 2000, p. 443)*

Children did recognize implicitly that things could be learnt through play: 'You learn to make stuff.' (child quoted in Keating *et al.*, 2000, p. 444). This wasn't a school 'thing'; school is the place for proper schoolwork to take place.

What are the implications for children who do not accomplish the 'real work' of the reception class quickly? How will they come to view themselves and others? These children see writing as 'real work', that is the thing that they have come to school to learn and at which they need to succeed. It counts. Yet around 46 per cent of six and seven year olds have difficulty with letter formation (Alston, 1995). By the time they are eleven years old, children will have spent thousands of hours, usually one-third of their time in class, involved in language-related handwriting tasks (Alston, 1995). At this stage 20 per cent of boys and 10 per cent of girls report that they 'hated writing' and, in addition, 37 per cent of boys and 23 per cent of girls claimed to write as little as possible and only when they had to do so (Alston, 1995; Sheehy and Jenkin, 1999). This situation will affect children's attitudes to themselves and their relationship to learning.

Already at an early age therefore some pupils are beginning to feel that the things they can do in school are not valued and that they are in some way 'outside' the valued groups. John Davis and Nick Watson have shown that this process of exclusion takes place in both

*Playing isn't work.*

mainstream and special schools. They found that children in special schools picked up adult perceptions and 'mirrored adult discourses'; when a child in a special school was asked the question 'Why are you here?', their answer was 'Because I'm not very bright' (Davis and Watson, 2001).

## How older pupils view school

For older children the work of school becomes less important in itself. Research that explored Scottish secondary school pupils' ideas about why they went to school revealed that for many pupils school served primarily as a social experience during the first two years and then later was seen as being instrumental in what would happen in their future lives:

> 'You don't want to be one of these drunks and that you see on the streets every day selling "The Big Issue".'
>
> 'You'll no get a decent job if you've no got any brains.'
>
> 'Now it's only four years, you'll go to university and then get a life.'
>
> *(Pupils quoted in Duffield, Allan, Turner and Morris, 2000, p. 266)*

For these young people, school was just something to get through. Their perceptions of school suggested that it had largely instrumental goals. Getting through school was about learning the correct performance. Pupils who found this difficult felt 'excluded by factors beyond their control' (Duffield *et al.*, 2000, p. 271) and excluded from participation in their own learning. Others were aware of how social influences affected their learning:

> 'It's better getting a bad mark then you dinnae get slagged as much ... [I want to be] just in between – about what everybody else gets, not do too well.'
>
> 'Some people say if you come from [area] and you get good marks ... or speak differently then you're a snob – when I first came to this school I was scared of a lot of people ... now I just ignore them – say shut up ... it's not my friends that do it, just people I don't like.'
>
> *(Pupils quoted in Duffield* et al., *2000, p. 268)*

Resentments were aired by boys about extra help being given to girls or to those with 'special needs'. It is interesting to note that analysis of the distribution of 'help' within schools does reveal a gender bias and we will consider experiences of this next.

## Gender bias in experiences of education

Research shows that historically boys, in fact, were 70 per cent more likely to receive additional help than girls, when all other factors, such as academic test scores, behaviour ratings and family background, were equal (Sacker, Schoon and Bartley, 2001). There is also more recent evidence that this form of gender bias continues to exist (Daniels *et al.*, 1999, cited in Sacker *et al.*, 2001).

After looking at gender differences in a school chess club, Ingrid Galitis concluded that, even in our 'arguably enlightened age of gender awareness', schools continue to 'transmit and reinforce inequalities between the sexes, albeit in more subtle and less overt forms than in the past' (Galitis, 2002, p. 71). The following field observations, made in a streamed secondary context, illustrate the gendered experiences of pupils in PE lessons:

Leanna's team always comes last – she moves very slowly, and has difficulty with the games that involve a ball and/ or feature complex instructions. Jonathon is also on the losing team, and he is getting fed up, remarking at first to himself, and then publicly, 'this is a rubbish team'. Ken re-divides the children for the last game, into two teams. The game requires each pair of children to sit facing each other at a distance, race around the edge of the hall when their pair's turn comes, run into the middle, and kick a ball over one of the benches which have been upturned at the end of the 'ladder' of children. Leanna cries at first, because she doesn't understand what to do. I find myself at first thinking how damaging competition is, and how the problem here is that there have to be winners and losers. But then I find myself getting really into the competition, especially when the pairs are evenly matched – it's exciting. When all of the pairs have had a turn, Ken ends the lesson. As they line up, Karl notes to Iftekar that 'your team won because you were nearly all boys, our team only had two boys'.

*(George Holt quoted in Benjamin et al., 2002, p. 6)*

Gender, one aspect of identity, can be used to build or maintain exclusionary processes. Pupils themselves can act as inclusion 'gate keepers' (Allan, 1999) by allowing others into or excluding them from aspects of school life, social and curricula.

## Different classrooms, different experiences

The inclusive classroom is one that provides for the learning of a diverse range of children. The pupils in the above example were in streamed secondary education. The 1997 White Paper on education (DfEE, 1997a) supported the policy of streaming by attainment in primary schools. Doug McAvoy, a former leader of a teaching union, interpreted this as 'setting is good and mixed ability is bad' (McAvoy, 1997, cited in Lyle, 1999). The practice of setting is endorsed through the National Literacy Strategy and statements from Her Majesty's Inspectorate (Lyle, 1999). This practice has been encouraged despite a lack of research evidence to support it and without seeking the opinions of the children themselves. So what do children think of different groupings for learning? We turn to look at this next.

## Children's attitude to mixed-ability groupings

Sue Lyle interviewed children from a school in Swansea that had run a 'mixed ability' and 'mixed gender' project designed to improve pupils' literacy. The tasks in the project were designed so that pupils were collaboratively involved with the activities and texts being studied.

Children expressed the view that there were some benefits gained from working in this mixed-ability, collaborative way. One pupil explained this was '... because you get more information because people share ideas' (pupil quoted in Lyle, 1999, p. 289).

*Children working collaboratively.*

Pupils were also aware that they were learning a way of interacting with one another, particularly where disagreements arose:

> 'It was like team work.'
>
> 'You might have an idea and someone will say, "no, let's have this one", and then you all start arguing. Then you discuss it to come up with the best idea.'
>
> *(Pupils quoted in Lyle, 1999, p. 290)*

The children mentioned rules that were important for this way of working, such as 'give the others a chance' and 'be nice to each other'. They also said that they had made new friends as a result of this way of learning: 'We've got closer, because before we thought they were dorks and stupid but we realise that they really, really are ... nice' (pupil in Lyle, 1999, p. 292). Further, children said they learnt from both helping and being helped by others in the class. 'When asked if they thought their work would have been as good if they had worked on their own there were unanimous cries of, "No!", "No Way!"' (Lyle, 1999, p. 290).

This way of working seems to be valued by the children and to benefit them in several ways. The positive feelings expressed by the children about this way of working seem to fit with research that asked children about what makes them happy in school.

## What makes you happy at school?

### The importance of friendship

When children are asked about the things that are important in their experience of education one factor appears to be important above all others – friendship.

In a study of 2,527 children in 500 primary and secondary schools in one local education authority (LEA) in the north-west of England 62.8 per cent stated that happiness at school was the result of friendships (Whittaker, Kenworthy and Crabtree, 1998). This included best friends and also friendly teachers and other friendly pupils. Along with this, 'feeling safe, making other children happy and being trusted by others' also added to their happiness (Whittaker *et al.*, 1998).

'When everybody is kind and helpful and everybody are friends' Female, Year 6

'Playing nice' Female, Year 2

'Feeling safe' Female, Year 6

'When everybody else is happy' Female, Year 6

*(Whittaker* et al., *1998)*

### The effect of bullying

When asked about what makes them unhappy the most commonly cited factor was bullying, either directly of themselves or of others within the school. Children gave the following reasons for feeling unhappy:

'When people make fun of me' Male, Year 6

'Being called [names] for something you can't help ... being shy' Female, Year 10

'Being told off and called names by the teacher and friends' Male, Year 6

'When you hear about other pupils that are being bullied' Female, Year 10

'When people pick on me and call me fat' Female, Year 6

'Not fitting in' Female, Year 6

'The teacher asks for suggestions and I put my hand up all the time and never get asked once ...' Male, Year 5

*(Whittaker* et al., *1998)*

### Feeling safe and secure in school

As we noted above, children place importance on feeling safe and secure. This desire could be used as an argument both in favour of and against inclusive education. It is a fundamental characteristic of most conceptualizations of inclusive schools that they are places where all children can feel secure about being themselves. Opponents of inclusion might argue, though, that a fundamental problem in mixing children together is that they may be exposed to situations where they feel and experience the opposite of this.

This leads us to ask the question: how can schools develop this aspect of school life and counter experiences of isolation and bullying? In a survey of English primary and secondary schools, Audrey Osler (2000) asked children for positive suggestions about reducing bullying. Two factors were raised consistently: teacher–pupil relationships and the ability to participate in school life. Pupils suggested that teachers should:

- give praise for good behaviour;

- listen to pupils;

- take trouble to sort out the underlying causes of disputes instead of just dealing with the immediate effects of violent behaviour;

- recognize bullying, racial and sexual-name calling and abuse as real problems among pupils;

- care more;

- investigate before they punish;

- show respect for all pupils.

*(Osler, 2000, p. 54)*

 ## Activity 7.3   Comparing viewpoints, understanding perspectives

Think back over the children's voices and their views of their experiences of education that we have read so far in this section.

How do your own views, as an adult, compare to those of these children?

Can you think of any other factors that might influence how they see school and their own place in school?

What are the implications of the pupils' views that we have discussed in this section for education in segregated settings, and for grouping and streaming?

Write down your thoughts in your learning journal.

This activity will help develop some of the skills needed for TMA 02 and the ECA.

 The children seemed to respond well to collaborative experiences, positive interpersonal relationships and a 'safe' school environment. School ethos, the ways teachers work with classes and the social setting of the school would all influence the extent to which children could become active participants in their own school lives.

## School councils

Audrey Osler also found that children were keen to become more actively involved in their schools and had a strong sense of their responsibility to the school community. Where they existed, school councils were seen by children as indicating 'a listening school'. They were also seen as a way for pupils' priorities to be presented to the decision-making bodies of the school. Osler identified a further significant benefit:

> as one of the primary schools demonstrated, a class council has the potential to offer peer support to vulnerable children or those at risk of contravening school rules. Thus, indirectly, they may help reduce the use of exclusion as a disciplinary sanction.
>
> *(Osler, 2000, p. 62)*

School councils appear to have merit in that they provide a forum for the expression of children's voices. It has been argued, however, that to be effective pupils need training to ensure that they represent accurately the needs of fellow pupils. Without this, participatory democracy can turn into tokenism or non-participation (Hart, 1992, cited in Carter and Osler, 2000). Furthermore it is important that pupils are not simply given areas where they are 'allowed' to contribute but must be able to choose areas where they feel change is necessary and understand the system enough to make a meaningful contribution.

##  Activity 7.4   How influential are children's voices?

Over the next few days we'd like you to observe occasions on which children are allowed to comment on and give their views about situations and issues. These might be situations in your own home or family circle, or scenes that you observe in public or in the media. You could do this in the form of rough notes jotted down on the move. Note the situation and issues concerned and when, and where, their voices are expressed. What audience can they be seen as addressing? Consider how far their voices are accorded power and granted validity in these situations.

* * * * * * * * * * * * * * * * * * * * *

At the beginning of the unit we started with the conviction that listening to diverse voices is central to our view of what inclusive education is and that attitudes to education are shaped by the society around us. In this section we have then given some perceptions that indicate that children can become passive non-participants in their education and that the instrumental nature of their learning distances them from what they themselves are doing and also from their peers. Segregation by ability seems to be linked to this. Furthermore, experiences of mixing and collaborating with other pupils brings contrasting experiences and feelings of participation and worth. If we are to develop inclusive schools we need to include and give importance to children's voices and enhance their participation as active learners and members of the school community.

## Into the mainstream?

### Children's views from inside

During recent years more disabled children have begun to attend mainstream schools. As you might expect, their experiences vary greatly. This range is illustrated by the following pupils' comments on their secondary schooling in Ireland.

> 'It was nice being with the normal crowd. It was just around the corner and I liked it and I put my name down, that's how I got to go there.'
>
> 'You had to fight. One girl had spina bifida. She couldn't handle the crowds; there were 1200 in the school. She left.'
>
> 'In science, using things on the bench, I just sat down and watched. I think most of us were excluded especially in sports – the school wasn't equipped to cope. They tried, but the majority of times you had to stay out.'
>
> 'We'd pair up, and my partner used to do all the physical work.'
>
> *(Shevlin, 2000, p. 4)*

The next two extracts were part of a research symposium entitled 'Human Rights, Inclusion and the Voices of the Oppressed' (Rieser, 2000). Two pupils gave their personal perspectives on issues related to inclusion. Both speakers are representatives of Young & Powerful, the

*Inclusive schools are places where all children can feel secure about being themselves.*

self-advocacy group of young disabled people that we introduced earlier in the course. The pupils have experience of inclusion and exclusion and are able to offer an 'insider's viewpoint' on both.

> My name is Chloe McCollum. I am 16 years old and have Down's syndrome. I love parties, having drinks, going to the market, stories and ET.
>
> I went to Lucas Vale, an ordinary primary school. I liked it there. I had many friends especially Nejula, Siobahn and Ellie. When I left Lucas Vale (after nine years) I wasn't allowed to go to ordinary secondary school with my friends. I campaigned to go, but the education authority said no. I stayed at home and my daddy taught me reading. He took me to museums and we had picnics together. I now go to Greenvale special school with kids my own age. I go to Deptford Green one day a week too.
>
> Deptford Green is a mainstream secondary school with lots of children in it. I love it because it is good there. I like reading especially a book called 'Underground to Canada'. I like writing, Science, Maths, English and Humanities. I like the experiments best. I play with everyone in the playground. It's great to go to an ordinary school and I like both my schools.
>
> I wish I went to Deptford Green after Lucas Vale and there wasn't such bother. I hope there won't be such bother for children in the future.
>
> *(McCollum quoted in Rieser, 2000)*

In the next extract Katherine Kephalas (aged 17) relates her experiences:

My experience of education has been I attended a mainstream school until I was no longer able to. My school was not inclusive for me due to the fact that they were not able to be flexible and the school campus was not accessible. This has meant that I have two hours a week with a home tutor. I no longer have the social contact that school gives and I have only kept up with my very closest friends. Even if I had only been able to go for five minutes a week I would have felt included. Instead I am excluded. My name is not read out at registration. It is as if I was never there.

... Disabled children do not exist in isolation, they exist as part of families and communities. If you exclude one part you exclude all the rest. It has made me come to the conclusion that we don't just experience segregated special schools, we experience segregated mainstream schools. All children are losing out through exclusion. The education system shows children a warped view of life – exclusion – which they then take into the adult world ...

*(Kephalas quoted in Rieser, 2000, p. 19)*

These extracts from Chloe McCollum's and Katherine Kephalas's presentations highlight the personal consequences of inclusion and exclusion and the importance that these young people give to inclusion. Both pupils present very clear positions about what they require from their education. Katherine's point about 'segregated mainstream schools' is a strong one which Young & Powerful has presented to government policy makers. In the process of moving towards inclusive education, the voices of pupils who have experience of segregation need to be heard. It is vital to know what they value about their education, and how they feel about the process of change and the changes that are necessary for them to feel included (Cook, Swain and French, 2001).

## 'Real men don't need rights'

If we are approaching the development of inclusive education from a human rights standpoint then pupils' rights need to be a part of a school culture that young people, not just adults and rights campaigners, are aware of. Charlotte Carter and Audrey Osler (2000) interviewed boys after they had engaged in a programme of problem solving based on human rights. The boys' opinions about this way of approaching issues were considered. The boys did not use rights as a part of their everyday discourse and most felt that rights were synonymous with 'needs and weaknesses'. They did not, therefore, like to talk about their own rights within the existing school set-up. The idea seemed to go against the culture of the school. 'If I had to say to someone I have a right to that, I would feel like I was asking their permission, they'd get the chance to say "no" and then I would look stupid' (pupil quoted in Carter and Osler, 2000, p. 345).

For these boys, needs and rights were confused and seen as not being masculine, that is, not the way that a man should approach things. Carter and Osler (2000) concluded that little solidarity existed amongst the pupils in protecting the rights of other children. Consequently, a boy who claimed a right 'within a context of inequality and fear' (p. 347) was seen as admitting powerlessness.

The rights agenda was also seen as being open to abuse either by teachers, in order to control pupils unfairly, or by pupils who might exploit their rights and 'push' teachers unfairly. In Carter and Osler's interview data no pupil, or member of staff, used the words 'rights and responsibilities' together. They concluded that it was essential to develop understanding of the concepts of responsibilities and trust if rights were to be openly discussed and acted upon in a participatory way. Such trust clearly needed to develop: 'They don't trust us to do anything properly. They treat us like babies and haven't even let us try. They don't want us to succeed, then they might have to treat us properly' (pupil, Carter and Osler, 2000, p. 347).

Pupils and staff remain distanced from one another within this system. If human rights are to feature explicitly in our development of inclusive education then they cannot simply be 'tacked on' to a system that separates pupils and staff in this way. Citizenship education has been mentioned as a possible way of endorsing the ideas of pupil participation and pupil perspectives in schools (Rudduck and Flutter, 2000). Citizenship education could make a considerable contribution to an inclusive school ethos and to how children regard their rights. It would seem to make sense that in order to empower children to participate effectively in society they should be given the experience of the principles of citizenship within their own schools. As Hodgkin argues, 'Democracy ... is not something which is "taught", it is something which is practised' (Hodgkin, 1998, quoted in Rudduck and Flutter, 2000).

In creating inclusive schools the communities of learners, parents and staff need to build particular relationships with each other. The video material of the Pen Green Centre and Bannockburn learning settings tackle this task and promote the acceptance of difference and diversity.

## A model for an inclusive school community

Charlotte Carter and Audrey Osler (2000) propose a model for developing a school community that is based on a human rights framework (see Figure 7.2). They suggest that this type of structure allows all members of the school to develop the confidence and skills to participate democratically. There is a strong link between children's and teachers' active participation in education and how they

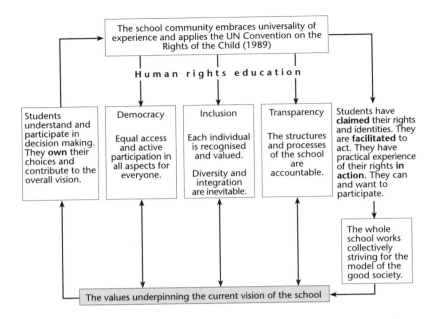

*Figure 7.2    Diagram showing the realization of the UN Convention on the Rights of the Child (1989) within a school community (Carter and Osler, 2000, p. 353).*

'construct' their own identities and those of their peers. Notice how their model includes the explicit teaching of human rights and an introduction of democratic processes. In this model democracy and inclusion are part of a flexible and responsive system that allows all members of the school community to 'access their rights and claim their identities' (Carter and Osler, 2000, p. 354).

## Activity 7.5   A democratic school

How might people respond to the idea of a democratic school? Explain the concept of a school based on human rights to a friend. Listen to their views of your explanation and discuss how they see democracy in relation to education.

Our view of inclusive education includes the need to listen to children and young people, firstly at a personal level, secondly in order to improve our educational practices in a variety of ways, and thirdly as an acknowledgement of pupils' human rights. As the 'consumers of education' we should at least find out what children and young people think about the education they receive. In this section of the unit, we have included their voices to give an insight into their perspectives on issues that they, as well as adult commentators, have identified as being important to inclusion. Whittaker *et al.* (1998) argue that, although children's participation may be dismissed by some as trivial or impractical, 'such views should be valued as an integral part of educational planning, delivery and decision-making at all levels' (Whittaker *et al.*, 1998).

A pupil in the Carter and Osler research commented:

> One of this school's major faults is the lack of voice a student is given. Some teachers forget we are growing up and just expect the childish things of little kids ... Some of the teachers are afraid to give a student the chance to explain himself.
>
> *(Carter and Osler, 2000, p. 347)*

There is certainly evidence that children and young people, when given the opportunity, are capable of commenting on issues that are relevant to their lives. Moreover, as we have seen in Unit 4, children's participation in decision making has become an integral part of government policy development. Campaigners for inclusive education, who argue strongly for more participation by young people, may therefore be pushing against an open door.

It is also important that we are aware of our own motivations in listening to children. 'Are we "using" pupils to serve the narrow ends of a grades-obsessed society rather than "empowering" them by offering them greater agency in their schools?' (Rudduck and Flutter, 2000, p. 82). Whilst this unit would, hopefully, not represent such an approach, the position put forward by us as authors is not a neutral one. You may wish to consider the motivation behind the selection of views presented in the unit so far. Can you envisage a situation where the motivations expressed here would be at odds with the desires of children and their parents? Some examples of such a conflict are seen in the next section, which focuses on the perspectives of parents.

# 3  Perspectives of parents

At first glance parents appear to have a much stronger voice in education than the pupils do. For example, if we looked only at government documents, we would be likely to conclude that, since the publication of the Warnock Report in 1978, parents have become increasingly important participants in decisions about additional educational provision. Legislation from 1981 to 2001 increased their statutory right to participate in decision making, not only through their direct contributions to assessment but also by way of appeals against LEA decisions. We would also see that during this time parent-led groups contributed vigorously to the lobbying that brought about strengthened rights to mainstream provision, introduced in 2001 in the Special Educational Needs and Disability Act (SENDA). In addition, in 1997 and again in 2001 challenges from parents and their allies in campaigning organizations have led to the withdrawal of government proposals which would have weakened the legal entitlements of children described in law as having 'special educational needs'.

In this final section of the unit we examine what 'parental participation' really means and the extent to which parents of children with additional needs are, in practice, included in the education system. We also look at what parents understand by the term 'inclusive education' and what they want for their children. We look at how the discourses that we have considered earlier in the course in relation to children and young people also have a parallel impact on parents. Parents, as well as children, experience the deficit-based medical model, and equally it makes them feel like failures. They also experience what Sheila Riddell and her colleagues (Riddell, Brown and Duffield, 1994, p. 331) have called 'benign discretion' at the hands of professionals, in which they find themselves marginalized and their parental knowledge discounted. Those who want their children to participate fully in mainstream education find themselves struggling to remove their children from 'care'.

Like a number of marginalized groups, parents have had to claim their right to participation. Sometimes they have claimed their rights as individuals, through the courts. Sometimes it has been through collaborating with pressure groups, alongside other parents or allies. How far they have been able to progress towards full participation has often varied according to their social class, gender or ethnicity, because of discriminatory pressures and processes.

Listening to the views of parents reveals that not all of them have a commitment to inclusive education; some parents do in fact prefer, for a range of reasons, to identify with a medical model. But for those struggling for more inclusive practices, their vision of inclusive education is one shared across national boundaries, as we shall see in Activity 7.8 where we read of the Hartmann family's story.

## Partnership – reality or rhetoric?

### The official position

The 1978 Warnock Report stressed the importance of working on equal terms with parents:

> We have insisted throughout this report that the successful education of children with special educational needs is dependent upon the full involvement of their parents: indeed, unless the parents are seen as equal

*Parents collecting children after school.*

partners in the educational process the purpose of our report will be frustrated.

*(DES, 1978, p. 150)*

The Warnock Report urged professionals to 'take note of what [parents] say and how they express their needs and treat their contribution as intrinsically important' (DES, 1978, para. 9.6).

The 1981 Education Act, which followed the Warnock Report, created a statutory right for parents to participate in the statementing process. In wording that has remained the same in both the 1993 and 1996 Education Acts, a legal duty was placed on LEAs to inform parents

*A parents' evening at school.*

when they proposed to make an assessment of the child's needs. At the same time, the LEA should inform the parent of their 'right to make representations and to submit written evidence'. Parents' legal rights were strengthened by the 1993 Education Act, which created rights of appeal to the independent Special Educational Needs Tribunal. Parental rights were further extended in 2001 by the introduction of a parental appeal right when LEAs refused a *school's* request for formal assessment. In addition, changes in legislation in 2001 created a statutory duty for LEAs to arrange for parents to be given advice and information, and LEAs were further required to arrange dispute resolution services, which included an independent element, and to publicize these services to parents and schools.

Alongside these changes to the law, other non-statutory government documents emphasized the central role of parents. The 2001 *Special Educational Needs Code of Practice* included a complete chapter on 'Working in partnership with parents' (DfES, 2001a). The accompanying *SEN Toolkit* devoted a complete booklet to 'Parent Partnership Services' (DfES, 2001b). The DfES publication *Special Educational Needs (SEN): a guide for parents and carers* tells its audience that one of its basic principles is that 'your views should be taken into account and the wishes of your child should be listened to' (DfES, 2001c, p. 3). The booklet goes on to say, 'Remember – you know your child better than anyone' (DfES, 2001c, p. 7).

The changes introduced by the 2001 Act may bring about greater participation by parents. However, despite the apparent strengthening of the legal role of parents between 1981 and 2001, in practice many of them continued to find participation in the special education system very difficult. Sheila Riddell and her colleagues, writing about Scotland in 1990, commented that statutory powers were still weighted in favour of education authorities. Little had been done, in their view, to promote parents' active participation; although parents wished to be involved in assessment, many had little idea of how this could happen (Riddell, Dyer and Thomson, 1990). As we have already seen in Unit 4, research in England reflected a similar situation, as parents described their need for support in order to make their case at the Special Educational Needs Tribunal (Andrews, 1996).

## Participation in practice

Parents may have been given rights in law, but relatively few have claimed them or, apparently, even know they are there. In a research project which looked at how LEAs enable parents to participate in statutory assessment, Sheila Wolfendale found that only 3 out of 67 of the LEAs she studied told parents in their documentation that they had a legal duty to provide advice for parents. Only half positively and strongly encouraged parents to send in their views and a quarter provided only weak encouragement (Wolfendale, 1997). Not surprisingly, the response to the opportunity to participate in assessment has not been equal across different groups. For example, articulate parents, who might be seen as taking a consumerist approach, may engage in the process more assertively, while other groups, such as parents from minority ethnic backgrounds, may remain marginalized in the decision making (Diniz, 1999). This trend is also seen in who gets additional support (Sacker et al., 2001).

## Activity 7.6 Children with serious medical conditions

Read the following chapter:

- Chapter 3, 'Child and parent relationships with teachers in schools responsible for the education of children with serious medical conditions', by Claire Norris and Alison Closs, in Reader 2.

In this chapter the authors discuss the experiences of children with long-term illnesses who can find themselves marginalized in the education system. Parents describe what support they need to continue to feel included.

In your learning journal divide a page into two columns, with the following headings:

- factors that led to the marginalization of parents or children;
- factors that promoted positive inclusive experiences.

As you read the chapter note down the factors you come across. When you have finished reading and making notes, think back to the earlier units of this course and try to relate the factors that you have identified with some of the models we discussed.

 When you have finished reading and making notes look at the table below, which shows some of the points that we noted. You may have found more.

| Factors that led to the marginalization of parents or children | Factors that promoted positive inclusive experiences |
|---|---|
| Teacher uncertainty | Acceptance of diversity |
| Fear of illness or death | Empathy with parent and child |
| Over-protectiveness | Respect for the pupil |
| 'Expert' professional views | Acceptance of parent views |
| Views of what is 'the norm' in terms of academic progress | Willingness to home visit |

In terms of positive inclusive practices, Claire Norris and Alison Closs found that what made the difference was not the nature of the child's illness or disability but the attitude of teachers and school staff. The medical model of disability led to negative attitudes, where teachers focused on what the child could not do. Furthermore, the medical model established the professionals as 'expert', a view that led to the undervaluing of the expertise and experience that parents could offer. Some 'professional' responses may well have sprung from fear and uncertainty. Some teachers acted counterproductively by becoming too preoccupied with care, rather than with challenging the pupil in an appropriately academic way. For some teachers, looking after a sick child can seem more important than providing access to education. Parents, on the other hand, were anxious for education to continue.

Successful inclusive practice, in contrast, involved the breaking down of traditional barriers, for example when teachers made home visits to encourage continuity if children had times of extended absence. Acceptance and respect for diversity, and a willingness to engage with the pupil on their own terms and to accept the knowledge held by parents, were the hallmarks of successful inclusive practice.

## Parents on the margins

We can see the medical model and the charity model in action in many of the accounts that parents have given of their experience. Eileen Gascoigne, herself the parent of a disabled child, writes about how parents can feel 'blamed' for 'what is wrong' with their child (Gascoigne, 1995). She gives the following illustration in which a mother describes how she had been made to feel responsible for the 'deficits' of her son, N, who had Asperger's syndrome:

> Fact: N had not bonded. Cause: it was my inadequacy as a mother – he didn't fail to bond with me, *I* had not bonded with *him*.
>
> Fact: N had not started talking. Cause: it must be my fault for not talking to him enough, not reading out loud to him enough.
>
> Fact: N did not relate well to others. Cause: it must be because I had not mixed enough with mother and toddler groups, coffee mornings, playgroups.
>
> Fact: N could not cope with change. Cause: clearly I had been too wedded to routine, or too prone to impulsive changes of routine.
>
> Fact: N has fixated behaviour. Cause: well, that *must* be my fault for not providing a diversity of stimulation for him in his early months and years.
>
> *(Mother quoted in Gascoigne, 1995, p. 13)*

The view that N's difficulties arose out of an individual deficit has led to a sense of deficit in his mother – she feels that professionals see N's difficulties as stemming from 'something wrong' with her. Another mother had a similar view:

> It got to the point where I couldn't go into the playground to collect V, because I knew his teacher would call me over to tell me what he'd done today. I got fed up with the constant negative. No one was suggesting solutions; I felt I was being blamed. OK, I know he is a bit difficult at times. But if I have difficulty at home with him, I sort it out. I don't expect to be called in for every little misdemeanour in the classroom: they should sort that out. And they never told me anything good, what he

had achieved or succeeded at, only what he'd done that
was bad. You can only take so much negative all the time.

*(Mother quoted in Gascoigne, 1995, p. 17)*

Pippa Murray, another parent of a disabled child, has written
powerfully about her experiences. She describes the way that she was
marginalized and made to feel 'different' (Murray, 2000). She links the
way she was treated as a parent with the way that society in general
views disabled people. For example, other people saw her loving
emotions as a parent for her child as in some way heroic, or unusual,
since they saw the disabled child as intrinsically unlovable. Pippa
Murray is sceptical about the view of 'partnership with parents'
promoted by government documents. She sees choice as being
integral to partnership; it seems to her that there has been little choice
in the relationships that she has had with professionals. Her
experience has been that the professionals she encountered,
influenced by the deficit model of disability, saw themselves in the role
of experts, so that her own experience was discounted. She notes that
the only real partnerships she formed were with her son's support
workers, 'professionals with the lowest status, least power and, in our
particular case, the least professional experience' (Murray, 2000,
p. 684).

Pippa Murray is a member of Parents with Attitude, a group that we
have met before in Unit 4. She is articulate and well informed: the
article that we have just discussed appeared in a respected academic
journal and gives her address as the University of Sheffield, where she
was a full-time PhD student. Nevertheless, in her roles as an academic
and parent, she feels marginalized and powerless.

## How parents experience exclusion

### Gendered experiences

Parents may experience additional forms of exclusion. You may have
noted that most of the parents' stories in this unit and in previous
units come from mothers. It is often mothers who take on the primary
caring role for a disabled child, and consequently it is often mothers
who attend meetings, for example to discuss school placements.
Within LEAs, senior officers are often male. Gender, and related
perceptions of power, may well be an excluding factor in parents'
dealings with predominantly male LEA officers.

### Social background and approaches to statements

Carol Vincent and her colleagues have shown how social class and
ethnic distinctions, and the divisions and stereotypes related to these
that exist in wider society, have an impact on the experience of
parents who seek additional help for their child. She records an
interview with a psychologist about the administration of the
statementing process:

We do tend to find ourselves with two sets of statements, one when we know there is going to be a difficulty with litigation and appeals and that sort of thing, which we do write in a very full manner, perhaps going into two or three pages ... because we know we are going to be challenged in a legalistic fashion ... You are making a pre-judgement on the basis of the interview with the parents that they're going to be a bit stroppy and therefore we've got to watch it. So it gets treated differently. I wouldn't say particularly they get more by being stroppy ... (but) it probably does (mean that). I mean if you were to look at it, you'd probably find that they have in fact achieved more, these kind of parents, but we try to keep a balance.

*(Psychologist quoted in Vincent, 1996, p. 479)*

As Carol Vincent comments, ' "These kind of parents" is a euphemism for mainly middle-class parents who have the necessary resources to challenge and dispute with officialdom' (Vincent, 1996, p. 479). Jean Gross, an educational psychologist employed by an LEA, noted a direct relationship between the length of written representations made by parents in the statementing process and the amount of resources allocated to their children (Gross, 1996). In her view, children with what she calls 'middle-class' special needs – needs that are not related to poverty or social class, such as Down's syndrome or sensory impairment – were 'overfunded' as a direct consequence of active advocacy by their parents. In contrast, children with emotional and behavioural difficulties and those with moderate learning difficulties, who were more likely to come from homes experiencing social disadvantage, were not equally well represented and as a result were 'underfunded' (Gross, 1996, p. 4).

## Minority ethnic experiences of exclusion

The exclusion that is imposed on disabled people can be further compounded by minority ethnicity and associated cultural, religious and linguistic dimensions. Whilst communication with teachers is a common problem affecting the parents of deaf children (Jones, Atkin and Ahmad, 2001) this communication is further reduced where there is a language barrier. 'It is difficult to understand my child's education because I don't know English. My husband used to go and speak to them, but I have no knowledge about what went on' (Maryam Fiaz quoted in Jones *et al.*, 2001, p. 66).

Lesley Jones and her colleagues (2001) asked Asian parents of deaf children about their perceptions of the services they encountered. One theme was the marginalization of their religious and cultural values. Schools did not give pupils space to express these. Salma Jabeen, mother of a thirteen-year-old deaf son, commented on the lack of religious education:

> ... school has told him nothing about religion. I would
> like a Muslim member of staff at the school. I have asked
> them but the head teacher said they can't afford it. It
> would be nice to have someone who could teach him
> about Islam ... They don't celebrate Eid, even though
> there are other Muslims there. That's why I say if there
> was a Muslim member of staff, they would do something,
> but at the moment there is nothing at all.
>
> *(Salma Jabeen quoted in Jones et al., 2001, p. 66)*

Parents, in the research of Jones *et al.*, believed that services designed
for deaf pupils needed to recognize and respond to cultural diversity.
Failure to do this was partly attributed to racism:

> When it comes to English people, they can get things
> done. The social workers are scared of them. But I swear to
> God, they take advantage of Asian people, because we
> don't know about anything, we can't speak English, so
> they take whatever advantage they can of us.
>
> *(Salma Jabeen quoted in Jones et al., 2001, pp. 66–7)*

Parents expressed a desire for a system that can recognize cultural
diversity. This recognition is essential if participation is to be achieved.

Pippa Murray comments that the parent's voice is ' small and, in the
end, insignificant in the face of the power of the professionals backed
by the legislation and the legislative process' (Murray, 2000, p. 691).

## Parents campaigning for change

You saw from your reading of the chapter by Claire Norris and Alison
Closs that parents have clear views about what is needed to bring
about positive and inclusive educational experiences. Good
relationships between teachers and parents were seen by the parents
in their study as crucial, along with willingness on the part of teachers
to acknowledge and value parental input. Raising awareness among
teachers was put forward as central to good practice, particularly as
the writers saw poor practice arising largely from the lingering impact
of a deficit, 'pathologized' model of disability.

Pippa Murray shares similar views to those of Claire Norris and Alison
Closs, but expands on their understanding of the central role of the
child. The real issue for her was the value placed on respect for her
son, a respect which enabled some professionals to accept him as he
was and 'to value and enjoy him without wanting him to change in
order that he fit into the current educational system' (Murray, 2000, p.
696).

Pippa Murray describes the confusion that arose in the early years of
her son's life because of conflict between her natural bond with her
son and the negative views that she met, not only in others, but also
in her own thinking about disability. The growing influence of the
adult disability rights movement helped her, eventually, to

understand the origins of her negative perceptions: 'I was fortunate that my early years of parenting coincided with the time that disabled adults were developing and publicising the social model of disability which states that people with impairment are disabled, not by their bodies, but by society' (Murray, 2000, p. 696).

*The disability rights approach has been instrumental in encouraging parents and children to claim their educational rights.*

The disability rights movement, by shifting the focus away from individual failure to a broader socially-based understanding of equality, difference and diversity, has had a major impact on the way parents have viewed themselves. Micheline Mason, a disabled parent, writer, and campaigner on disability rights issues, makes a specific link between the disability rights movement, young people and parents:

> I was born with a condition called Osteogenesis Imperfecta, or 'Brittle Bones'. I am neither ashamed nor particularly proud of this as it was not of my choosing. What I am very proud of is the kind of person that dealing with this challenge has *enabled* me to become. I think I am a wiser, deeper, richer and more competent person than I would have been had I not had this challenge put before me. I have also had the privilege of close contact with many others who have had similarly enriched experiences of life – my friends at school, my sisters and brothers in the Disability Movement, my own wonderful daughter. I treasure this.

Our aim is to alter the way people feel about the word
'disabled' from a negative attitude to a positive attitude,
in exactly the same way that 'Black' has to be a positive
assertion of identity in a racist society ...

For young people it is essential that they somehow make a
connection with those of us who have – at last – forged a
positive sense of identity as disabled people. This is also
important for teachers and parents.

*(Rieser and Mason, 1992, p. 22)*

Parent groups, such as Parents with Attitude, often closely allied to the
disability rights movement, have been one avenue which parents
have used to press for a more inclusive education system. The
influence of the disability rights movement is clear in, for example,
the manifesto of Parents with Attitude, as set out on its website:

Parents with Attitude is committed to making visible the
experience of disabled children and their families from a
human rights perspective. Our work centres around the
belief that our disabled children do not have to be
changed or fixed; that all our children are ordinary
children just as they are; that it is the experience offered
by a disabling world that does not give them ordinary
lives.

*(Parents with Attitude, 2002)*

Another campaigning organization is Parents for Inclusion (formerly
Parents in Partnership). Alice Paige-Smith comments that the change
of name, in 1996, was brought about in order to recognize that '"true"
partnership with professionals is not possible, as professionals have
the power to exclude children against the wishes of parents and the
child' (Paige-Smith, 1997, p. 48). As well as campaigning, Parents for
Inclusion also offers advice to parents.

Alice Paige-Smith describes the growth of parent organizations
following the 1981 Education Act. One such organization, Network
81, was founded by parents Liz and David Arrondelle, whose daughter
Kirsty had Down's syndrome. Starting from a base in the Arrondelles'
own home, by 1991 the group had achieved charitable status and
funding from Children in Need. By the time Alice Paige-Smith was
writing in 1997, the group had 500 members and 67 local groups
affiliated to them, 30 of which were local Network 81 groups. 'While
the group does not campaign by "waving banners", according to the
national co-ordinator, the group encourages parents to go out and
question how LEAs respond to their requests for the provision they
want for their child' (Paige-Smith, 1997, p. 49). Network 81 also offers
an advice line to parents.

For many parent groups, campaigning and consciousness-raising is
allied to giving information. Access to information, for example on
the legal framework surrounding children described as having 'special

educational needs', can be an empowering experience for parents. In an article about parent participation in annual reviews, Phyllis Jones and John Swain point out the importance of parents understanding the minutiae of the statement of special educational needs: 'In the experience of these parents, the more detailed and specific the Statement, the greater its potential power in affecting the educational decision making in relation to their child' (Jones and Swain, 2001, p. 63).

As we saw in Unit 4, the extent to which statements contribute to the development of inclusive practice is an area of heated debate. For some campaigners, the statementing process and the Special Educational Needs Tribunal are simply an example of the oppression of disabled people, and as such to be treated with contempt. However, some parents equally committed to inclusion have seen the statement as a crucial factor in securing an inclusive placement. Action on Entitlement, an umbrella group of very diverse groups which is both parent-led and for parents, came together in 1998 to challenge what they saw as a threat to children's rights to provision contained in the 1997 Green Paper, *Excellence for All Children* (DfEE, 1997b). In 2000, they campaigned against the Government proposal which would have changed regulations and weakened the role of statements in the allocation of resources for individual children. Parents for Inclusion, the Alliance for Inclusive Education, the Centre for Studies in Inclusive Education and Network 81 were all part of their campaign. Their campaign material included case studies of the way inclusive placements had been adversely affected by vague statements. One such example is presented in the box that follows.

### Lauren

Lauren was born with a rare genetic disorder which has given rise to learning difficulties. Her mother wanted her **placed in a mainstream school, with support, and to be educated alongside children without disabilities**. Lauren's statement named her local school but was vague about the arrangements and the amount of support she should receive in the classroom:

> 'Access to a mainstream setting with support to enable Lauren to utilise her strengths and skills ... Support at Level 6 on the Matrix to assist the head teacher in the planning and implementation of suitable work programmes.

During Lauren's second year at school there were problems with the level of learning support she received in the classroom. When her mother raised this as an issue, she was told by the class teacher that it was difficult to meet Lauren's needs with the resources available. The head teacher and SENCO, however, claimed that she was already receiving more help than her statement entitled her to. In truth, the statement was too vaguely worded for anyone to know what exactly had been intended.

Nevertheless, Lauren's mother and the school agreed to ask the LEA to increase the Matrix Level, the 'ladder' of provision established by their LEA. The LEA agreed, and issued an amended statement to this effect as from the beginning of this school year. But they still refused to specify how much help Lauren should receive. Then, quite suddenly, the school began withdrawing Lauren from the classroom for four mornings a week, to be taught in a small group with two other children who have severe learning difficulties. Lauren began imitating their behaviour and stopped making progress with her social development. Her mother complained but was told that, due to the vagueness of the statement, the school could arrange her provision in any way they saw fit.

In July 2001, the Government withdrew their proposals, but securing appropriate funding for their child still depends on the initiative and energy of individual parents. It is this individually based approach to funding that has been seen by some commentators as being at odds with the development of inclusive provision, since they see a tension between the rights of individual children and the overall funding available to schools in general.

As we have noted elsewhere in the unit, and in Jean Gross's work from an LEA perspective in particular, individually based funding can tie up resources with those children whose parents are most articulate and confident. Such parents do not necessarily want inclusive placements for their children, as Sheila Riddell and her colleagues showed in their study of dyslexia groups in Scotland. These parents actively supported a medical model of learning difficulty and distanced themselves from others:

> The secretaries of the local branches of the Dyslexia Association emphasised their view that children with specific learning difficulties should not be regarded as part of the continuum of learning difficulties; they were a distinct and separate group whose problems were qualitatively different from those of other children with learning difficulties.

> (Riddell et al., 1990, p. 335)

A parent was anxious to underline differences between children with dyslexia and those with more global learning difficulties, saying: 'There is a comparison/lumping together of dyslexic children and those who are mentally retarded. Dyslexic children are NOT MENTALLY RETARDED' (parent quoted in Riddell *et al.*, 1990, p. 336).

Riddell *et al.* commented that organizations that supported parents attempted to 'shift the general paradigm away from a curriculum-deficit model of learning difficulties back towards a child-deficit model, to enable children with specific learning difficulties to be regarded as essentially different from those with more global problems' (Riddell *et al.*, 1990, p. 339). In doing that, Riddell *et al.* also commented that:

> These parents and the supporting voluntary organisations were acting legitimately in pursuit of their individual and collective interest. They made it clear that they were speaking only for their own interests and, indeed, were willing to pitch their claims against those of other pupils with different learning difficulties ... The Scottish Dyslexia Association ... may, indeed, have had the effect of diverting resources away from other children with learning difficulties through the effectiveness of its campaigning.

> *(Riddell* et al., *1994, pp. 341–2)*

You will have your own views on this tension between individual rights and the interests of a larger group.

## Activity 7.7   Representing children

Find two campaigning parental groups, for example through an internet search, leaflets from a local library or an advertisement. Note how the groups represent their children in relation to other children. What means do the groups use to raise the profile of their own children?

A fundamental issue that emerges for us in this unit is how fairly the law is applied. The real challenge, for voluntary agencies and for parent partnership schemes, is to enable less confident and marginalized parents to participate on equal terms. Advocacy has a major role to play in enabling marginalized groups to claim the rights that exist for all.

In many cases where individual parents have sought to use the law to bring about an inclusive placement for their child, what was under discussion was not the amount of money being spent, but where that money was spent. The Crane family from Lancashire, for example, whose story you will look at in more detail in Unit 15 of the course, argued that in fact a mainstream placement would have saved

Lancashire LEA money. They argued that a special school placement, with associated taxi costs, would have cost the LEA much more than a properly resourced placement in their local secondary school (Brandon, 1997, p. 123).

The justification of efficient use of resources was advanced in a case in the US, where the Hartmann family, like the Cranes in Lancashire, sought to reinstate their 11-year-old autistic son in a mainstream classroom in Loudoun County, Virginia.

## Activity 7.8   Making the news

First read to page 277 in the following chapter:

- Chapter 23, 'The news of inclusive education: a narrative analysis' by Bruce Dorries and Beth Haller, in Reader 1.

The story of Mark Hartmann led to intense correspondence in local and national papers in the US. Once you have read this first section, taking the perspective of a parent, a professional or an interested observer, draft your own 500-word letter to the local paper.

After completing your draft, finish reading the rest of the chapter, which analyses the themes that came up in the media coverage of this story.

Now go back and look at the letter you drafted. Where would your response fit, in terms of these narrative themes? Does your response cover more than one theme?

This activity will help develop some of the skills needed for TMA 02.

In this part of the unit we have looked at the experiences of parents of disabled children and seen how they, like their children, are likely to be marginalized or viewed in the light of particular models of disability. We have seen how parents have responded to this marginalization, by joining together and, in particular, by learning from the experiences of the adult disability rights movement. We have looked at how parents have used the law, with varying degrees of success, to support their attempts to bring about a more inclusive education system. Finally, we have noted that, although the law is based on individual cases, the struggle for inclusive education both in the UK and elsewhere can generally be seen not as a simple struggle to secure resources for a particular child, but as part of a wider struggle for equality and for acceptance of difference and diversity.

# 4 Conclusion

This unit has presented and discussed the voices of different people, primarily pupils and parents, and has used them to help build a positive perspective concerning inclusive education. We suggest that factors such as gender, ethnicity and social class all impinge upon and interact with people's ability to access inclusive education provision. The perspectives of pupils and parents reflect these influences as well as their overt concerns with disability and access to education.

You may take a different approach to these perspectives. If you were writing this unit you might have chosen a different range of voices and experiences, and reached a different conclusion. TMA 02 and TMA 04 will give you an opportunity to comment on issues that have been raised in this unit.

By listening to and considering the voices expressed here, we hope that you will have developed your own perspective further and deepened your understanding of some of the factors which influence the development and implementation of inclusive education. Throughout this unit we have argued that an inclusive system is one that is democratic and respects human rights. This includes the right for people to be heard and to be actively involved in the decisions that affect their own lives.

# References

Allan, J. (1999) *Actively Seeking Inclusion: pupils with special needs in mainstream schools*, London, Falmer Press.

Alston, J. (1995) *Assessing and Promoting Writing Skills*, Stafford, NASEN Enterprises Ltd.

Andrews, E. (1996) *Representing Parents at the Special Educational Needs Tribunal*, Marlow, IPSEA.

Armstrong, D. (1995) *Power and Partnership in Education: parents, children and special educational needs*, London, Routledge.

Aspis, S. (2001) 'Inclusive education, politics and the struggle for change' in Barton, L. (ed.) *Disability, Politics and the Struggle for Change*, London, David Fulton.

Atkinson, D., Jackson, M. and Walmsley, J. (1997) *Forgotten Lives: exploring the history of learning disability*, Kidderminster, British Institute of Learning Disabilities.

Barton, L. (1997) 'Inclusive education: romantic, subversive or realistic?', *International Journal of Inclusive Education*, 1(3), pp. 231–42.

Benjamin, S., Nind, M., Hall, K., Collins, J. and Sheehy, K. (2002) 'Moments of inclusion and exclusion: pupils negotiating classroom contexts', paper presented at British Educational Research Association Conference, Exeter, September 2002.

Brandon, S. (1997) 'The invisible wall: Niki's fight to be included', Hesketh Bank, Parents with Attitude.

Carter, C. and Osler, A. (2000) 'Human rights, identities and conflict management: a study of school culture as experienced through classroom relationships', *Cambridge Journal of Education*, **30**(3), pp. 335–56.

Cook, T., Swain, J. and French, S. (2001) 'Voices from segregated schooling: towards an inclusive education system', *Disability & Society*, 16(2), 2001, pp. 293–310.

Davis, J. M. and Watson, N. (2001) 'Where are the children's experiences? Analysing social and cultural exclusion in "special" and "mainstream" schools', *Disability & Society*, **16**(5), pp. 671–87.

Department for Education and Employment (1997a). *Excellence in Schools*, Command paper CM/3681, London, HMSO.

Department for Education and Employment (1997b) *Excellence for All: meeting special educational needs*, London, DfEE (Green Paper). Available from: http://www.dfes.gov.uk/sengp/foreword.shtml (accessed November 2003).

Department for Education and Skills (DfES) (2001a) *Special Educational Needs Code of Practice*, London, DfES.

Department for Education and Skills (DfES) (2001b) *SEN Toolkit*, DfES, London.

Department for Education and Skills (DfES) (2001c) *Special Educational Needs (SEN): a guide for parents and carers*, London, DfES.

Department of Education and Science (DES) (1978) *Special Educational Needs: Report of the Committee of Enquiry into the Education of Handicapped Children and Young People* London, HMSO (the Warnock Report).

Diniz, F.A. (1999) 'Race and special educational needs in the 1990s', *British Journal of Special Education*, **26**(4), pp. 213–17.

Duffield, J., Allan, J., Turner, E. and Morris, B. (2000) 'Pupils' voices on achievement: an alternative to the standards agenda', *Cambridge Journal of Education*, **30**(2).

Farrell, A., Taylor, C., Tennent, L. and Gahan, D. (2002) 'Listening to children: a study of child and family services', *Early Years: the Journal of International Research and Development*, **22**(1), pp. 27–38.

Froese, P., Richardson, M., Romer, L.T. and Swank, M. (1999) 'Comparing opinions of people with developmental disabilities and significant persons in their lives using the individual supports identification system (ISIS)', *Disability & Society*, **14**(6), pp. 831–43.

Galitis, I. (2002) 'Stalemate: girls and a mixed-gender chess club', *Gender and Education*, **14**(1), pp. 71—83.

Gascoigne, E. (1995) *Working with Parents as Partners in SEN*, London, David Fulton.

Gross, J. (1996) 'The weight of the evidence: parental advocacy and resource allocation to children with statements of special educational need,' *Support for Learning*, **11**(1), pp. 3–8.

Hancock, R. and Mansfield, M. (2002) 'The literacy hour: a case for listening to children', *The Curriculum Journal*, **13**(2), pp. 183–200.

Harrett, J. (2002) 'Young children talking: an investigation into the personal stories of Key Stage One infants', *Early Years: the Journal of International Research and Development*, **22**(1), pp. 19–26.

Jones, L., Atkin, K. and Ahmad, W. I. U. (2001) 'Disability and supporting Asian Deaf young people and their families: the role of professionals and services', *Disability & Society*, **16**(1), pp. 51–70.

Jones, P. and Swain, J. (2001) 'Parents reviewing Annual Reviews', *British Journal of Special Education*, **28**(2), pp. 60–4.

Keating, I., Fabian, H., Jordan, P., Mavers, D., Roberts, J. (2000) 'Well, I've not done any work today, I don't know why I came to school: perceptions of play in the reception class', *Educational Studies*, **26**(4), pp. 437–54.

Kenworthy, J. and Whittaker, J. (2000) 'Anything to declare? The struggle for inclusive education and children's rights', *Disability & Society*, **15**(2), pp. 219–31.

Lyle, S. (1999) 'An investigation of pupil perceptions of mixed-ability grouping to enhance literacy in children aged 9–10', *Educational Studies*, **25**(3), pp. 283–96.

Murray, P. (2000) 'Disabled children, parents and professionals: partnership on whose terms?', *Disability & Society*, **15**(4), pp. 683–98.

Osler, A. (2000) 'Children's rights, responsibilities and understandings of school discipline', *Research Papers in Education*, **15**(1), pp. 49–67.

Paige-Smith, A. (1997) 'The rise and impact of the parental lobby: including voluntary groups and the education of children with learning difficulties or disabilities' in Wolfendale, S. (ed.) *Working with Parents of SEN Children after the Code of Practice*, London, David Fulton.

Parents with Attitude (2002) Parents with Attitude website. Available from: http://www.parentswithattitude.fsnet.co.uk [accessed March 2002].

Riddell, S., Brown, S. and Duffield, J. (1994) 'Parental power and special educational needs: the case of specific learning difficulties', *British Educational Research Journal*, **20**(3), pp. 327–44.

Riddell, S., Dyer, S. and Thomson, G. O. B. (1990) 'Parents, professionals and social welfare models: the implementation of the

Education (Scotland) Act 1981', *European Journal of Special Needs Education*, **5**(2), pp. 96–111.

Rieser, R. (2000) 'Human rights, inclusion and the voice of the oppressed' [online]. Paper presented at International Special Education Congress 2000: Including the Excluded, University of Manchester. Available from: http://www.isec2000.org.uk/abstracts/papers_r/reiser_r_l.htm [accessed 12 January 2003].

Rieser, R. and Mason, M. (1992) 'Disability equality in the classroom: a human rights issue' in *Disability Equality in Education*, London, Disability Equality in Education.

Rudduck, J. and Flutter, J. (2000) 'Pupil participation and pupil perspectives: "carving a new order of experience" ', *Cambridge Journal of Education*, **30**(1).

Sacker, A., Schoon, I. and Bartley, M. (2001) 'Sources of bias in special needs provision in mainstream primary schools: evidence from two British cohort studies', *European Journal of Special Needs Education*, **16**(3), pp. 259–76.

Sheehy, K. and Jenkin, L. (1999) 'An evaluation of the Teodorescu Perceptuo-Motor Programme of Handwriting', *REACH: The Journal of Special Needs Education in Ireland*, **13**(1), pp. 35–47.

Shevlin, M. (2000) 'Hidden Voices: young people with disabilities speak about their second level schooling'. Paper presented at International Special Education Congress 2000: Including the Excluded, University of Manchester.

Vincent, C., Evans, J., Lunt, I. and Young, P. (1996) 'Professionals under pressure: the administration of special education in a changing context', *British Educational Research Journal*, **22**(4), pp. 475–91.

Whittaker, J., Kenworthy, J. and Crabtree, C. (1998) 'What children say about school', Bolton Data for Inclusion Data, 24, September 1998. Available from: http://www.inclusion-boltondata.org.uk/FrontPage/data24.htm (accessed October 2003).

Wolfendale, S. (1997) 'Encouraging parental views as part of statutory assessment: an analysis of local authorities special educational needs documentation produced for parents', *Support for Learning*, **12**(3), pp. 99–103.

# UNIT 8   Professional perspectives

*Prepared for the course team by Mary Kellett and Kieron Sheehy*

## Contents

# 1 Introduction

In this unit we explore the perspectives of professionals on inclusion and what their roles entail. To do this it is necessary to have some understanding of curricular and pedagogical (teaching and learning) issues and classroom dynamics. Therefore this unit begins with a discussion of these issues in inclusive education. We then take a closer look at some of the key professional roles in the school environment.

Schools need many different approaches to enable teachers to educate a diverse range of learners in one and the same classroom (Corbett, 2001). They may need to make physical changes to the learning environment and employ additional adult support, and usually they have to adapt the curriculum. Some argue that it also involves accessing specialist teaching skills (e.g. Hornby and Kidd, 2001), whereas others claim that no special set of methods is needed (e.g. Thomas and Loxley, 2001). These opposing viewpoints illustrate deep-rooted tensions that exist in different approaches to inclusion and learning.

Throughout the unit we emphasize curricula provision and classroom practice based on learning *diversity*. Our focus is on the total learning environment rather than individual 'need' or 'difficulty'.

## Learning outcomes

By the end of this unit you will:

- have an understanding of classroom practice issues relating to diversity and inclusion;

- have an appreciation of some of the professional roles in inclusive education and how these roles interrelate;

- be able to critically appraise the different perspectives of professionals as stakeholders and their impact on inclusive education;

- be able to relate the material in this unit to the video material in Unit 5, reflecting on how these professional perspectives affect the practical environment of the classroom.

## Resources for this unit

For Activity 8.3, you will need to read:

- Chapter 18 in Reader 2, 'Learning without limits' by Susan Hart.

For Activity 8.8, you will need to read:

- Chapter 19 in Reader 1, 'Learning support assistants talk about inclusion' by Caroline Roaf.

# 2 Curricula and pedagogy: the building blocks

Jerome Bruner (1993, p. 413) claims that 'any subject can be taught effectively in some intellectually honest form to any child at any stage of development' and Tina Bruce (1991) reminds us that we can teach chemistry to three year olds if we think of it in terms of finger painting! It is all a matter of degree. So, beginning with the premise that *all* children are capable of *some* learning, *what* should teachers be teaching and *how* should they be teaching it? The perspectives that different professionals hold on these questions are shaped by the relationship between their beliefs and their professional roles and identities. Often beliefs about fundamental aspects of learning are taken for granted and assumed to be shared by everyone. We consider three of these aspects now and highlight potential contrasts between them (derived from Reeves, 1997).

## Three questions about learning

### (a)   What is knowledge?

Objectivism ⟵——————————————⟶ Constructivism

Beliefs about the nature of knowledge can be seen as spanning a continuum. At one end is 'objectivism'. This viewpoint sees knowledge as something that exists independently of people. There are pre-existing truths and these are waiting for us to discover them. Learning is about discovering these truths and how much we have learned can be measured precisely using tests.

At the other end of the continuum is 'constructivism'. This asserts that people build knowledge themselves, based on their prior experiences and social interactions. Constructivist teaching enables students to build their own ideas. For example, in science lessons students may be given the opportunity to 'rediscover' currently accepted theories through experimentation and collaboration.

### (b)   How do students learn?

Instructivist ⟵——————————————⟶ Constructivist

Setting precise goals and objectives independent of the learners is an example of an instructivist approach. Objectives are set out in the sequence in which they are to be learned. The student follows this sequence. The content of what the student should learn is determined beforehand and the teaching focuses on pouring this content 'into' the student, as if s/he were an empty jar that needed filling.

Constructivist methods begin with the learner, perhaps involving their interests and motivations, presenting them with a range of experiences. Of prime concern in this philosophy is whether a person's behaviour or their thinking is targeted. It aims to develop problem-solving skills and strategies for investigation. For example, in medical education some training schools use a problem-solving approach to learning, alternating this with clinical experience. This approach contrasts with the traditional one of several years of fact memorization followed by a clinical placement (Perlemen, 1992, cited in Reeves, 1997).

### (c)   What should the teacher's role be?

Expert $\longleftarrow$ $\longrightarrow$ Helper

The 'traditional teacher' role has been didactic, that is, teaching through the presentation of information to pupils. This approach depends on a power relationship: the teachers have status because they know important things which they can pass on to pupils, who lack power because they don't know them. Increased access to information through the internet, however, has challenged the necessity of the teacher as the only mediator of knowledge.

## ▷ Activity 8.1

You may have formed an opinion already about this course and the way that it presents information and activities. Where would you place it on each of these three dimensions? Note down brief comments on this in your learning journal. This will give you an analysis of how knowledge and learning are seen in this course. It will also offer you a framework for looking at the examples of inclusive practice within this unit.

## What do we teach in an inclusive environment?

At one time the justification for all children not learning together was that they needed different curricula. The introduction of the national curriculum in England and Wales in 1989 moved this debate on, however, in that access to the same curriculum became the entitlement of *all* pupils. Special schools that previously enjoyed large amounts of freedom over choice of curricula now had to adapt the national curriculum for their pupils.

The following extract describes how Manjula, a seven year old with profound and multiple learning difficulties, is able to engage in a positive way with the national curriculum. The extract describes how a school visit to a cathedral was linked to religious education, geography and history in key stage 1 of the national curriculum.

It is hard for her teacher and caregivers to know when Manjula is learning because she does not use speech or any kind of sign language. However, by including her in the visit to the cathedral they are providing her with important experiences, shared with other children. In fact, these experiences give Manjula the opportunity to show that she is aware of important things during the visit. Sitting in her wheelchair, beneath the cathedral's Rose Window, Manjula is left for a few minutes to look, listen, and feel where she is. As the sun shines through the window, Manjula smiles and wrings her hands with pleasure. Back in school, Manjula's teacher and learning support assistant help her to make a 'sensory' picture book as part of a topic on the cathedral. They make her a personal tape of the kind of organ music heard during the visit. This brings learning to life for Manjula, and brings other real benefits. Some of her classmates also enjoy the organ music and the class teacher organizes a small 'listening group'. Manjula's mother and father, when they hear about this successful activity, decide to make her a tape of Buddhist chants used in their community temple. Thereafter, whenever the family visits the temple, they play the tape in the car and Manjula gets very excited with anticipation. The curriculum experience described here has been well matched to Manjula's needs, and importantly, this has been 'negotiated' on the basis of her response to an activity. She might have been left out of the school visit, but instead she was included and showed her educators, friends and family that she was developing a seemingly new awareness that could help her develop valuable choice making skills.

*(Tilstone et al., 2000, p. 14)*

There is widespread debate about whether an adapted national curriculum is appropriate for all pupils, particularly for pupils with profound and complex learning difficulties. On the one hand it is a powerful recognition of the common humanity of all children and their right not to be excluded from the curriculum. On the other hand, a 'one-curriculum approach' may be inhibiting for some groups of children if it prevents time being spent on essential life skills or alternative teaching approaches or therapies. The need for some curriculum diversity was recognized by the Dearing Report (SCAA, 1994) and flexibility has been increasingly built into the national curriculum (DfES, 2003). The onus has shifted to use of the national curriculum in ways teachers judge to be relevant.

Ensuring that the curriculum is relevant for disabled pupils continues to be a challenge. The British Deaf Association has lobbied the government to recognize British Sign Language as a 'first language' and an integral part of England and Wales' national curriculum. A curriculum that recognizes that pupils may be of any age when working towards level 1 is continually sought. As a step towards this, some teachers have welcomed the preparatory ('P') scales introduced by the Qualifications and Curriculum Association (QCA) in 1998 (DfEE, 2001). Debate on curriculum inclusion and diversification continues to rage with occasional guidelines offered.

The inclusivity of curriculum initiatives presents major challenges for professionals. The literacy and numeracy strategies introduced to primary schools in England in 1998 and 1999 respectively received a mixed response. Some teachers see the strategies as a retrograde step towards narrow prescription and others have reported that they have made literacy and numeracy more accessible to some groups of learners.

The curriculum encompasses both what is taught and how it is taught. It is significant in demonstrating the kinds of knowledge that are valued. For professionals working in schools decisions have to be made in terms of:

- how to value the 'home' knowledge of a great diversity of learners;
- how to map curriculum entitlement to individual pupils and their individual learning styles;
- how to provide opportunities in the curriculum for a diverse range of needs to be met at individual, group and whole-class level.

## How do we teach in an inclusive environment?

From our constructivist approach, curriculum content is not something simply transferred from teacher to pupil, but needs active engagement in the learning process. It has been assumed that how one engages a pupil in the curriculum depends on their particular impairment or 'special need'. Ann Lewis and Brahm Norwich (2000) evaluate the arguments behind this assumption and reject the case for distinct pedagogies for particular kinds of learning difficulties.

Likewise, Christina Tilstone *et al.* (2000) maintain that teaching children with different needs does not demand specialist teaching, just *good* teaching. Central to good teaching for all is:

- acknowledging different learning styles;
- 'scaffolding' the learning process (providing initial support to a student, which is gradually removed);
- differentiating on the basis of individual diversity;
- appreciating speech and language diversity;
- diversification.

We now explore these five themes.

## Acknowledging different learner styles

Pupils have different personalities and prior experiences and perceive and process information in different ways, sometimes described as a range of learning styles. Teachers should attempt to fit their teaching to their pupils' learning styles rather than the other way round. In practical terms this often means adjusting the environment (for example, quiet, changed lighting, seating patterns) or using a combination of different presentation and activity styles (such as talking, seeing, doing).

## Activity 8.2

Some examples of different learning styles are summarized in the box below. It is one way to help teachers step outside their own styles to appreciate that learners may be different from them – but no style is right or better. Before you look at the box, jot down a few characteristics about how you learned something yourself, for instance how you learned to drive or how you approached Unit 1. If possible, share your thoughts with another student. Now compare your notes to the descriptions in the box. Do you identify with any of these styles? Is your learning style very different? How similar is your learning approach to that of a friend or colleague?

| | |
|---|---|
| **Impulsive** | rushes at a task without stopping to think first |
| **Reflective** | chews over a task, sometimes endlessly |
| **Extrovert** | outgoing, gregarious learner |
| **Introvert** | the 'private' learner who prefers to keep to her/himself |
| **Holist** | needs to get a quick, overall picture before filling in details |
| **Serialist** | prefers to build up a picture methodically and analytically |
| **Field dependent** | solves problems from a context |
| **Field independent** | works from a stimulus rather than a context |
| **Scanner** | makes a general hypothesis then processes information as to how it fits the hypothesis |
| **Focuser** | tests several variables before forming a conclusion |
| **Divergent** | uses inspirational flair |
| **Convergent** | prefers closed situations and must find the 'right' answer |

*(Kellett, 1998)*

## Scaffolding the learning process

For some teachers and psychologists learning is something that happens almost entirely inside the child. The developmental theorist Jean Piaget suggested that children developed through a series of stages and that, because of this, there would be certain things that they could and couldn't do (Piaget and Inhelder, 1972). For example, he showed that young children couldn't 'conserve' (i.e. interpret as the same amount) an amount of liquid which had been transferred from one beaker to another, differently shaped, beaker.

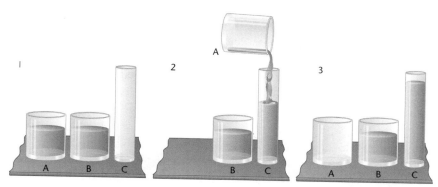

Figure 8.1    *A conservation of volume test. First a child identifies that Beakers A and B contain the same amount of liquid. Then the child watches as the liquid is transferred from A to C. Children at Piaget's 'pre-operational' stage will now judge that the amounts of liquid in B and C are different.*

This type of evidence suggested that there were limits to the things that children could learn and understand, and that these limits corresponded to the child's 'stage of development'. Although this may seem a reasonable assumption, teachers and parents were aware that children could function at much higher levels than those predicted by Piaget's stage theory.

Later re-investigation confirmed that under certain conditions young children could operate at levels well above that predicted by Piaget. For example, Light, Buckingham and Robbins (1979) produced a conservation task where pasta was transferred between two beakers of different sizes. As predicted by Piaget's theory, six-year-old children were unable to realize that the amount of pasta remained the same when moved to a beaker of a different size. However, when a reason was given for transferring the pasta shells, telling the children that the beaker was chipped, and therefore the pasta needed to be moved, a change occurred. With this simple addition the majority of children were now able to conserve, to realize that the amount of pasta remained the same.

The children in the pasta shells example appeared to have become 'cleverer'. However, we have seen that children can do more, and think things through in a more advanced way, if problems are presented in different ways. Simple changes in the environment enable children to understand concepts that might appear beyond them from a within-child learning perspective (Sheehy, 2000). One explanation for this is that children perform better when things make 'human sense', as Margaret Donaldson called it (Donaldson, 1978). This term expresses the relationship between social interaction and intellectual development. Children's learning largely takes place within a social situation and is actively developed by that social situation. The challenge for inclusive classrooms is to create a social situation that works for everyone.

Children's learning and understanding can extend beyond that which they are capable of reaching alone, when supported by the social environment. The difference between what children can do with and without this social support was referred to by Vygotsky as the 'zone of proximal [next] development'. Good teaching occurs within this zone, created by an enabling social environment.

This type of adult intervention is like the idea of 'scaffolding' (Bruner, 1985). Scaffolding occurs when a teacher supports the student in a task or activity. The support allows students to perform tasks that would normally be slightly beyond their ability without that assistance and guidance. Scaffolding is an important characteristic of constructivist learning and teaching, encompassing strategies such as modelling solutions, verbalizing thinking and providing feedback. It implies that a lot of what we are able to do is not located within ourselves. It is shared between us and the external resources that we use.

## Differentiation

One of the ways in which teachers can work with diverse learners is to differentiate the learning experience, that is, to make it different for different learners. Differentiation describes a range of techniques for matching learning experience to learning styles, abilities and competencies. Differentiation can also be used to create a good fit between learning experiences and varied life experiences, interests and cultures.

Some professionals view differentiation as two dimensional – differentiation by task or by outcome. This allows children to work on the same broad material but with different tasks and products. For example a worksheet may be differentiated for children with different reading skills. Figure 8.2 (overleaf) shows two examples of differentiated worksheets for a project on the Egyptians for pupils at key stage 2 (aged seven to eleven).

Returning to our three questions about learning (p. 136 ff), what model of knowledge is being used here? While some teachers rely heavily on this approach, others feel that this is effectively streaming and therefore stigmatizes certain pupils. In a project aiming to reduce stigma, Jonathan Rix and colleagues sought an alternative approach.

## EGYPTIANS AT HOME

1. Write the title - Egyptian Homes.

2. In the big box, draw an Egyptian's house.

3. In the the rest of the boxes, draw four things that you could find in an Egyptian's house.

## EGYPTIAN CLOTHES

1. Write the title - Egyptian Clothes.

2. In the left box, draw an Egyptian lady, showing the clothes she would wear.

3. In the right box, draw an Egyptian man, showing the clothes he would wear.

4. In the bottom box, draw three things the Egyptians would wear on their heads.

*Worksheet 2.*

---

## EGYPTIANS AT HOME

1. What were the Egyptian houses built out of?

2. Where did the Egyptians build their houses?

3. Describe what an Egyptian house looked like.

4. Which sort of buildings were built in stone?

5. What sort of furniture did the Egyptians have?

6. Where did the people do their cooking?

7. How were the houses of the rich different to the houses of ordinary people?

## EGYPTIAN CLOTHES

1. What were the Egyptians' clothes made of?

2. Why did they use this to make their clothes?

3. Why didn't every Egyptian wear brightly coloured clothes?

4. Describe the sorts of clothes Egyptian men wore.

5. Describe the sorts of clothes Egyptian women wore.

6. What did the children wear?

7. Describe what the Egyptians wore on their feet.

*Worksheet 1.*

*Figure 8.2   Differentiated worksheets for a project on the Egyptians.*

They wanted to support teachers working in secondary school classes that included many pupils at different levels of proficiency with English as an additional language (EAL). Rix comments:

> The traditionally recommended approach to such a situation is to produce differentiated materials; these are handed out at appropriate moments to those students deemed to need them. This procedure generates a number of significant issues, however. The most commonly observed issues were:
>
> - Some pupils for whom English is an additional language feel that they are being picked out from the majority unfairly. Some students with only English feel that they should be given the 'easy work' too.
> - These materials are difficult to produce in large quantities and the criteria governing their production are uncertain.
> - There is a misconception by the teaching staff that the production of differentiated materials and their distribution will alone satisfy the needs of the students.
> - Pupils for whom English is an additional language feel left out of the mainstream curricula up to the point at which 'their' materials appear which in turn engenders disaffection and resentment in teaching staff which reduces the value of the differentiated materials.
> - Pupils believe that they cannot do the work unless it is differentiated, a belief shared by teaching staff.
> - Confusion among teaching staff over the appropriate level of differentiation required by a specific student and across ability ranges.
> - Significant problems generated by rapid turnover and frequent new arrivals.
> - Problems of material ownership and the means by which differentiated materials can be shared and utilized by teaching staff using different styles, processes and mainstream materials.
>
> *(Rix, 2002, pp. 3–4)*

Rix and colleagues designed worksheets and activities that all pupils would work though – so they shared a common resource and starting point, but moved at different paces from there on.

Another strategy is differentiated support, which involves all learners working on the same task with different levels of support. Brian McGarvey and colleagues (1998) found a range of such methods of differentiation used in Northern Ireland. Most co-ordinators and teachers used a combination of four methods of differentiation:

Differentiation by task

Differentiation by outcome

Differentiation by resources

Differentiation by in-class support

Using different types of differentiation does not necessarily address the whole learning environment or the process of learning itself. It is dangerous to make assumptions about the kinds of differentiation that learners 'need'. Some education professionals resist differentiating the curriculum in favour of addressing the more complex learning environment.

## Activity 8.3

Now read Chapter 18 in Reader 2, 'Learning without limits' by Susan Hart.

As you read through this chapter identify the reasons that Julie gives for not using differentiated approaches in her work and the alternatives that she practices.

After reading the chapter, consider your own position on these arguments. Do you agree with all of them? Can you list arguments for and against the use of differentiated materials? Make a note of your ideas in your learning journal.

A key point that emerges is Julie's perspective on 'ability' and how children can be freed from imposed limitations. Differentiation is one way of imposing these limitations.

Alice Udvari-Solner and Jacqueline Thousand (1995) describe a model of inclusive classroom practice that combines core practices – good teaching for all – with adaptive strategies to meet unique needs. Core practices include focusing on what children can achieve, being responsive to different cultures, supporting peer tutoring and collaborative learning, and teachers collaborating together. Against this backdrop of everyday practices teachers constantly make decisions about what to adapt, adjust, streamline, expand and so on. Udvari-Solner and Thousand suggest that it is important that teachers do not over-adjust and make adaptations that are more intrusive than necessary. Therefore teachers need to ask themselves the following questions, in this order:

- Can the student actively participate in the lesson without modifications and will the same essential outcome be achieved? (*If so, don't adapt!*)

- Can the student's participation be increased by changing the instructional arrangements? (*For example, size and type of groupings, teacher-directed or student-centred learning.*)

- Can the student's participation be increased by changing the lesson format? (*For example, more experiential learning, more practical work.*)

- Can the student's participation and understanding be increased by changing the delivery of instruction or teaching style? (*For example, to match the learner's preferred style.*)

- Will the student need adapted curricular goals? (*For example, different complexity, depth, breadth.*)

- Can changes be made in the classroom environment or lesson location that will facilitate participation? (*For example, lighting, noise level, furniture layout.*)

- Will different instructional materials be needed to ensure participation? (*For example, texts, worksheets.*)

- Will personal assistance be needed to ensure participation? (*For example, support from another adult.*)

- Will an alternative activity need to be designed for the student and a small group of peers? (*For example, something related but activity-based or community-based.*)
  *(adapted from Udvari-Solner and Thousand, 1995, pp. 156–62)*

Udvari-Solner and Thousand see many alternatives to moving straight to differentiating the activity or the materials. They also see adult help, such as a one-to-one assistant, as close to a last resort. They regard it as better to use the natural supports of other learners and ordinary staff who are an unobtrusive part of the everyday routine. The model provides a problem-solving framework for teachers and highlights the many options open to them in responding to learner diversity. The decisions teachers make in relation to such options reflect their perspectives on knowledge, their role, their purpose, their students, and inclusive education.

## Speech and language diversity

I spent that first day picking holes in paper, then went home in a smouldering temper.

'What's the matter, love? Didn't you like school, then?'

'They never gave me the present.'

'Present? What present?'

'They said they'd give me a present.'

'Well, now, I'm sure they didn't.'

'They did! They said: "You're Laurie Lee, aren't you? Well just you sit there for the present." I sat there all day but I never got it. I ain't going back there again.'

*(Lee, 1962)*

Sometimes, teachers are so familiar with their environments and routines that they forget their pupils may not share their understanding. Children may use the same words as adults but their associated meanings can be very different (Sheehy, 2002).

Laurie Lee's teacher did not appreciate that 'for the present' was an idiom outside his experience. She needed to step outside her own frame of reference – to 'de-centre' – in order to understand his language differences. The more familiar something is, the harder it is to do this (Donaldson, 1978) and yet if we are to teach successfully in the inclusive classroom, the ability to de-centre is vitally important. For some the metaphors of classroom language can present a barrier to learning. This is highlighted by Ginulla Gerland and her experience of autism.

> ... to me it's not the big misunderstandings, the ones you read about in books on autism, that has been most difficult. Like, for example, misinterpreting 'Give me your hands' and thinking they want to chop them off.
>
> What has been very confusing and often hurtful are the more subtle ones, the ones that no one could ever explain. Like when someone said 'It's getting better' or 'of course you will get that job', and I thought this meant they actually knew this.

*(Gerland, quoted in Roth, 2002, p. 246)*

## ▷ Activity 8.4

Read the short extract below. It has been transcribed from a teacher's field notes and describes part of a maths lesson with Mike, an eight-year-old boy who had been identified by the school as having 'special educational needs'. As you read, try to imagine the feelings of (a) Mike, (b) the teacher, and (c) the other children in the group.

In our money topic today I was working with a small group of children on 'change from 10p'. I set up a pretend shop. The other children were coping well with buying and correctly predicting the amount of change: if, for example, they bought a fire engine for 7p, then they would get 3p change.

Mike, however, was floundering – buying the jigsaw puzzle for 9p prompted the answer of 5p change and the more times he tried the more bizarre his answers appeared to be, sometimes even more than the original 10p. I was puzzled because Mike had previously demonstrated competence in subtraction problems, and could work with numbers as big as 20. I wondered if he didn't understand the coin values, but on checking, found he could tell me what all the coin values were correctly.

We did some simple subtraction sums – 10 take away 6; 12 take away 4; 14 take away 8 – all of which he worked out correctly using the adding-on method with his fingers. So I gave him 10 1p coins instead of his 10p coin and asked him how much he would have left if he bought a paintbrush for 5p. Mike peeled off five pennies to give to me and then told me he had 5p left. Eureka! So we did some more. How much would he have left if he bought the rubber dinosaur for 8p, or the ruler for 7p, or the whistle for 3p? Mike worked them all out correctly, quickly and easily.

I took away the 10 pennies and gave him a single 10p coin back again. How much change would he need if he bought the stapler for 7p? Mike replied 20p! My elation bubble burst. It was only then that realization finally dawned on me. Perhaps Mike didn't understand what *change* meant! So I asked him what he thought change meant and he replied,

'It's when you change sommat for sommat else.'

'How do you mean, Mike?'

'Well, like swapping the 10p for sommat else, like for a 20 or a 5 or one of them (pointing to the coins on the table).'

Did the fact that you were told that Mike had 'special educational needs' influence the way you read the extract? Did you make any assumptions about his lack of understanding? This teacher recognizes that she failed to 'de-centre' like Laurie Lee's teacher. In fact, Mike did not have any conceptual difficulty with the maths at all, merely a different experience of language use.

## Diversification – the celebration of difference

Some teaching approaches, such as whole-class teaching, can be unresponsive to diversity. They are most unresponsive when they proceed along a prescribed script, which may or may not engage the range of learners, and which fails to alter to accommodate the pupils' various responses. The problem is the assumption that teachers must keep tight control over teaching planned for a group that is imagined to be homogeneous. In inclusive classrooms, however, lessons need to be diversified so that differences are not just taken into account, but celebrated. Comments from one teacher illustrate how her perspective on diversification was influenced by a conversation she had with her African-American friend, Tangye:

> 'How can I help the African-American boys in my class? They don't respect me. But I treat them like I treat all my white kids. I try not to look at their skin colour. I like all my students. I treat them all the same' ... Tangye almost stopped dead in her tracks ... she said affectionately, 'That's the problem. We don't want to be treated the same. We *are* different. We want you to acknowledge that.'
>
> *(Diller, 1999, p. 821)*

A more flexible and creative approach to the curriculum can foster racial inclusion and help reduce the high exclusion rates amongst black and minority ethnic groups (Appiah, 2000). Figures from the Social Exclusion Unit (1998) reveal that 16 per cent of excluded pupils were from minority ethnic groups and nearly half of that 16 per cent came from the African-Caribbean community although they made up only 1 per cent of the school population. Linda Appiah recommends that histories, languages, religions and cultures of Black and minority ethnic communities are incorporated into the curriculum. Diversifying the school experience means doing more to make multiracial and antiracist perspectives integral parts of school textbooks and schemes of work.

Diversification also involves open-ended tasks. Their open-ended character allows for all different kinds of participation, without a closed idea of what it is to succeed or fail. In open-ended activities, learners can bring their own experiences to bear in making sense of the task. They can use language and examples that are meaningful to them. They can make mistakes, seek clarification, observe peers and take risks. In order to make best use of this kind of diversification, however, teachers have to have a set of attitudes and beliefs that allow them to share control of the teaching and learning with their students.

## Summary

So far we have suggested that inclusive teaching involves a move away from 'within child' deficit thinking towards an acknowledgement of the importance of the learning environment, a shift of emphasis from learning *difficulty* to learning *diversity*. It requires a willingness to apply problem-solving strategies to adapt the curriculum and the teaching to the learner as opposed to requiring learners to fit into pre-specified and inflexible imparting of knowledge. We see the inclusive curriculum as one that adopts a constructivist stance and develops activities that are co-operative, interactive and meaningful.

# 3   Perspectives of key professionals

## Classroom teachers

> In the end, it is teachers who mediate policy through their activities in and out of the classroom, through their participation in the realization of curriculum.
>
> *(Clough, 1999, p. 67)*

It is teachers who are responsible for putting curricular and pedagogical approaches into practice. But 'teachers' in this sense have come to mean a whole range of professionals. There are learning support teachers (in Scotland), SENCOs (special educational needs co-ordinators in England, Wales and Northern Ireland), classroom teachers, support teachers, specialist teachers, student teachers, newly qualified teachers, and headteachers. We have teachers in classrooms, in resource bases, in pupil referral units, in mainstream schools and special schools, in community and residential settings. To what extent are teachers' perspectives on inclusion influenced by their specific teaching task, their immediate environment, their team colleagues and senior managers?

In the box overleaf are some examples of teachers talking about their experiences of inclusion taken from Thomas O'Donoghue and Ron Chalmers's (2000) study of how teachers manage their work in inclusive classrooms. The quotations indicate how complex and wide-ranging teachers' perspectives are. They highlight some of the operational/ideological conflicts we noted earlier and illustrate how teachers are adapting their working practices to facilitate greater inclusion.

---

'I have no doubt that inclusion is the right thing to do. The days of segregating children with disabilities are behind us. But teachers are going to need a lot of support and advice to make sure that all kids in the class get a fair deal.'
(Mary, p. 895)

'I was quite open with the deputy principal. I told him that I was setting up the classroom and establishing routines that would take care of Lucy's needs, but that I would be relying heavily on the teacher-aide to work with her. I am happy to put time into preparing her programme, but I can't take time away from all the other kids during class time.'
(Anne, p. 896)

'I think there will be more gains than losses for me in this [inclusion]. I've already learnt a lot of new things about my teaching so far this year. By making changes to the way I teach I am going to get more satisfaction and the class is going to work more effectively.'
(Joan, p. 896)

---

*(O'Donoghue and Chalmers, 2000)*

O'Donoghue and Chalmers identify three stages in the way teachers approach inclusion. The first of these is to focus on classroom organizational practices, the second is to consider adaptations to teaching strategies and the third is to explore how curriculum content can be adapted. Teachers, they say, move through these stages at different rates, some finding it difficult to move beyond the changes to classroom organizational practices. It is worth noting that this process does not explicitly include consultation with pupils.

There have been a number of studies of teacher perspectives (e.g. Scruggs and Mastropieri, 1996; Farrell, 1997; Jenkinson, 1997). Peter Mittler summarizes what such recent and current research tells us about teachers' attitudes to inclusion:

- most teachers in mainstream schools support the principle of inclusion but many have doubts about whether it would work in their school;
- teachers are much more positive about the inclusion of children with sensory or physical impairments than about those with emotional and behavioural difficulties or severe learning difficulties;

- Class teachers have less positive attitudes than head teachers but much depends on the credibility of visiting specialist support personnel; and
- support for inclusion generally increases once teachers have directly experienced it and they feel the scheme has the full support of the headteacher and local authorities.

*(Mittler, 2000, pp. 134–5)*

'Emotional and behavioural difficulties' rank high among teachers' concerns about inclusion and their own coping strategies (Forlin, 2001; Dyson, 2000). Many teachers fear that violent episodes might erupt in their classes and they will not be able to protect their pupils or themselves: '... I was worried about the safety issues. I kept on thinking about my responsibilities and what would happen if anything went wrong. I used to wake up at night worrying' (teacher Anthea, quoted in O'Donoghue and Chalmers, 2000, p. 901).

These are very understandable concerns for teachers and signal their need for strong team and management support. Teachers do not always find such support in their school. Phil Garner (2000) found that teachers often felt that their colleagues had a less positive view of 'EBD children' than themselves: 'I would be very anxious if our (school) drive for a more inclusive approach was left in the hands of _____ (named teacher) because he just does not see EBD pupils as having a rightful place here' (Garner, 2000, p. 3).

## Training issues: student and newly qualified teachers

With much inclusive thinking based on concepts of human rights and valuing difference it becomes clear that training for inclusion is not simply about focusing on the transfer of knowledge relating to various impairments or deficits. Training inclusive teachers involves more than repackaging special education practices under a new title. Instead, priorities include creating flexible learning environments, adaptation of materials and collaborative teaching and learning.

So, how does training measure up? Is enough being done to ensure that new teachers coming into the classroom are adequately prepared for inclusive teaching? Joanne Brownlee and Suzanne Carrington (2000) designed a study to help student teachers develop positive attitudes to disabled learners by providing them with structured opportunities to learn alongside Sarah, a student with cerebral palsy and communication difficulties. The student teachers commented on the richness of this learning experience:

> You have to get different people's perspectives on what is happening, although the tutors have worked with disabled people you have to get their [disabled people's] point of view as well about the subjects. It's really beneficial having someone [Sarah] like that in your class.

*(student teacher quoted in Brownlee and Carrington, 2000, p. 102)*

The student teachers compared this firsthand experience of inclusion to the formal preparation for inclusion they were experiencing on the teacher education programme:

> 'They have tried to cater for it [inclusion] in various subjects and fit it into how, if a situation were to arise … with a child in an inclusive setting, the ways of dealing with that. But I feel it's very limited and very general, and not specific enough.'

> … 'I think we need some practical experiences that will help us before we go. Apart from this [learning alongside Sarah], I haven't had any real personal experiences with disabled people at all. How am I meant to go out into the classroom and know how to interact or what support they are going to need or where to get support from?'

> *(student teachers quoted in Brownlee and Carrington, 2000, p. 103)*

The student teachers in the study also gave their opinions on how their course might better prepare them for inclusive education. Many of them said they would like more personal insights:

> Get a chance to spend time with somebody who's got a disability or somebody who is a teacher of a child with a disability, just to give us a few hints or just to talk to us about it. To sort of try and get rid of that feeling of what would I do?

> *(student teacher quoted in Brownlee and Carrington, 2000, p. 103)*

Student and newly qualified teachers sometimes face tensions trying to survive in environments where inclusion is only a veneer. Beneath the veneer contradictions may lie, such as high exclusion rates, exclusive grouping practices and closed attitudes to learning diversity. A lack of disabled teachers in schools is part of this veneer. Another example of it is how staff talk about children among themselves. Thomas and Loxley (2001) contrast the public and the private vocabulary used by staff to describe children (see Figure 8.3). 'Public use' equates with vocabulary staff are comfortable using with parents and unfamiliar professionals, 'private use' equates with vocabulary staff are comfortable using in informal discussions with familiar colleagues in the staff room.

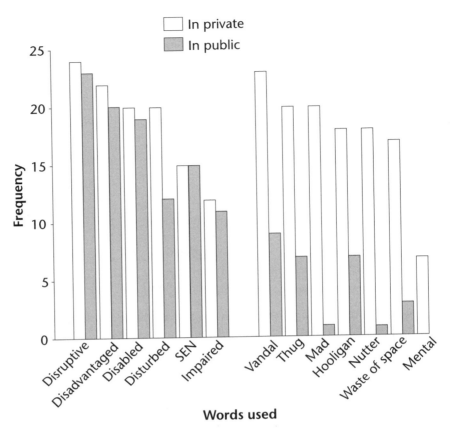

*Figure 8.3    Public and private vocabulary used to describe children (adapted from Thomas and Loxley, 2001, p.56).*

## Activity 8.5

Study the graph in Figure 8.3. Were you surprised by any of the data? Take a few minutes to reflect on the tensions for inexperienced teachers faced with similar staffroom dilemmas.

## Support teachers

One model of inclusive education involves support teachers (qualified teachers without a class responsibility) who are frequently allocated to individual pupils who are experiencing difficulties. The amount of withdrawal of pupils from the main body of the class, for individual or special tuition, is minimized. With greater numbers of pupils receiving support in the classroom environment, there are greater numbers of support teachers working alongside individual or small groups of pupils. Tensions can result where a support teacher is effectively a 'guest' in another teacher's lesson. This is particularly noticeable in secondary schools. Gary Thomas *et al.* (1998) reveal that support teachers often feel an 'acute sense of low status'. Pupils commonly regard them as student teachers or parent helpers. The class teacher retains overall control. Embarrassing situations sometimes arise such as a class teacher demanding, 'Who is talking?' only to discover that the noise is coming from discussions between the support teacher and pupil. This can inhibit free-flowing support especially if pupils are reprimanded for talking when they are trying to clarify something with their support teacher. Equally, class teachers may feel their teaching is under constant scrutiny from colleagues.

However, when support teachers are able to overcome these difficulties and work as part of a collaborative team with joint planning and evaluation, some powerfully effective inclusive education can result.

 ## Activity 8.6

Richard Rose (2001) interviewed twenty primary school teachers and seven head teachers, asking them to consider the implications of including two fictional pupils in their class.

---

Pupil A has poor co-ordination and his speech is indistinct. He can read a few words and count to twenty consistently but has difficulties with retaining information. He has a limited concentration span and feels the need to wander around the classroom, with a tendency to distract or interrupt other children.

Pupil B has cerebral palsy and uses a wheelchair. She has little physical control over her limbs and no speech though she can indicate 'yes' and 'no'. She uses a communication board with a head pointer, can read simple sentences and add and subtract single digit numbers. She needs help with all of her personal needs, including eating and going to the toilet. Regular medication controls her epilepsy although she has not had a major seizure for two years.

*(adapted from Rose, 2001, p. 150)*

There were five themes common to staff responses:

**Classroom support:** If pupils with special educational needs were to transfer from special schools it would be more likely to work if they came with support staff.

**Training:** Concern about lack of personal professional experience and the skills they would need to deal with children with special educational needs in their classrooms. Most said they felt very unprepared and that current levels of knowledge, understanding and practical skills were inadequate to support increased inclusion.

**Time issues:** A quarter of the teachers mentioned the extra time needed to prepare for children with special educational needs but only one head teacher saw this as an issue.

**Physical access:** Difficulties of access were noted in some teachers' classrooms e.g. one was on a first floor, others were too small to accommodate a wheelchair.

**Parental concerns:** Headteachers were concerned that parents would think pupils with special educational needs were monopolizing teachers' time. Parents would be worried that children with emotional and behavioural difficulties would provide a bad example or might harm their own child.

Do you think any of the problems raised are insurmountable? The term 'integration' might provoke exactly the same list. What kind of shift in thinking needs to happen to facilitate inclusion? Earlier in the unit you met evidence of teachers becoming increasingly supportive of inclusion once they had direct experience of it. The teachers in Rose's survey had not had any direct experience of inclusion. Compare their responses to the thinking of a teacher who did.

When asked to compare two children with disabilities with other children in her class she seemed oblivious to the kinds of concerns raised above, merely replying, 'All of my students are similar: they come to school expecting to learn, and they do learn; and each is unique in that they approach learning in their own individual way.'

*(Keefe, 1996, p. 6)*

# Team work

A recurring theme is that teachers are more effective and enthusiastic about inclusion when there is good team work. Team work occurs when there is a partnership among school personnel who work together as equals for the benefit of all the pupils in the class, pooling their expertise in content knowledge, teaching strategies, child development and practical knowledge of how to support children. Teachers' confidence about inclusion has been shown to be related to how much collaboration and support they receive in their own learning and training.

*Learning and Inclusion: the Cleves School experience* (Alderson, 1999) describes one primary school's approach to creating an inclusive school community. Priscilla Alderson notes the success of team work at Cleves:

> The 12 or 13 staff in each wing work as a team. Besides having their own base group of children, the four base teachers work with every child in the wing, spending two weeks in turn in the four main activity rooms ... Dividing up the preparation and teaching time among the team means that each session can have more staff time and attention than if one teacher covered the whole curriculum separately for each base group.
>
> *(Alderson, 1999, p. 18)*

> 'Here, there is much more adult interaction which is an absolute god-send at times because you can bounce off ideas and share problems. If one of us has discipline problems with a child, we can very easily pass them on to someone else, and it is like a clean slate. There's no aggression ... It definitely helps that this is a very supportive system to work in.'
>
> *(teacher Jim, quoted in Alderson, 1999, p. 18)*

Lara, who teachers pupils with English as an additional language, describes how she feels about the school's approach:

> 'Everyone is valued here, I think that's the big difference. Children who have recently arrived in England and do not yet speak much English are included as much as everyone else. They are encouraged to use English and their first language as well. I thought that would be a big job for me to get my colleagues to allow them to do this, give them opportunities to use their first language too, but it is not so here. There are displays here in first and second languages, and it is the ethos of the whole school,

not just a few individual teachers who might do that ...
Here, it is about equality, no matter who you are, what
you look like, what you do, we are all the same, we all
have something to contribute.'

*(Alderson, 1999, p. 40)*

## Special educational needs co-ordinators

The special educational needs co-ordinator (SENCO) role emerged in
response to the Education Act of 1993. The introduction of the Code of
Practice in 1994, and its revision in 2001, defined and refined SENCOs'
status and responsibilities. Caroline Roaf comments, 'the Code has
given SENCOs permission to be assertive and fulfil their role as
advocates for children' (Roaf, 1998, p. 114). Some SENCOs are part of
senior management teams and may have no class teaching
responsibilities. They can influence policy and practice at a senior
level, negotiating budgets and deploying resources and need
managerial, administrative and evaluative skills to carry out their
demanding role successfully.

The SENCO role has two main dimensions, one at a whole-school level
and the other at the level of the individual child. SENCOs divide their
time between working with individual pupils, advising and training
staff, liaising with other agencies and doing administrative tasks.
Some, such as Sarah quoted below, claim that their workload has
expanded to virtually unmanageable proportions, much of this from
a need for extensive liaison and the onerous statutory requirements of
the Code of Practice.

Roaf, herself a former SENCO in a comprehensive school, notes that
SENCOs increasingly act as promoters and facilitators of change in
respect of teaching and learning issues. She argues that their role has
three main facets: organization and management; research; and staff
development and training.

Roaf states that SENCOs are:

at the cutting edge of curriculum and staff development
every day. At Lord William's [Roaf's school], with learning
support assistants (LSAs) supporting nearly 20 per cent of
lessons, there is a constant dialogue of inquiry,
observation and assessment. This information contributes
to the school's research and development programme
supporting reflective teachers in a learning school.

*(Roaf, 1998, p. 120)*

The third facet, that of staff development and training, has grown
rapidly and extends to SENCOs' involvement in peer appraisal, team
teaching, and mutual support and observation as effective ways of
addressing the training needs of other staff.

# The individual education plan (IEP): a paper dinosaur?

One of the many 'bits of paper' that SENCOs need to deal with is the individual education plan (IEP). The intention is that education staff, parents and the pupil themselves jointly plan the IEP with specific targets for development and strategies for achieving them. The plans are reviewed termly or half-termly. Some teachers dislike IEPs because they are heavy on paperwork and targets can be unrealistic, unachievable or so small and bland as to be de-motivating. Many are unconvinced that they are effective, arguing that the time and cost of IEPs could be better used on direct support or resources for the identified pupil.

> If IEPs are driven by the need to fulfil external or internal bureaucratic demand, they will never impact upon a child's ability to learn and a teacher's ability to teach. If they are driven by the prioritized need of the child, they will demand that the curriculum is responsive to individuals.
>
> *(O'Brien, 1998, p. 149)*

Tim O'Brien proposes replacing IEPs for *some* 'special' children with ICPs (individual curriculum plans) for *all* children. This would highlight the 'C' part of the plan, the *curriculum*. O'Brien proposes a framework based on learning aims, objectives, routes, conditions and outcomes.

> An ICP would accommodate ... the variety of learning styles that we meet in our classrooms and provide more flexibility for individual progress ... It extends the potential of teachers and pupils to self-generate a curriculum which will offer incremental risk – releasing rather than controlling pupils – so that they can begin to understand their own learning styles.
>
> *(O'Brien, 1998, p. 149)*

 Activity 8.7

John Dwyfor Davies, Philip Garner and John Lee (1999) used 'concept maps' to elicit responses from SENCOs about their role. Each SENCO was asked to make a drawing which in their view best summarized their role, and then provide a brief written explanation of their drawing. Figures 8.4 and 8.5 show two examples of these concept maps. Look at each concept map and try to work out what the SENCO was communicating.

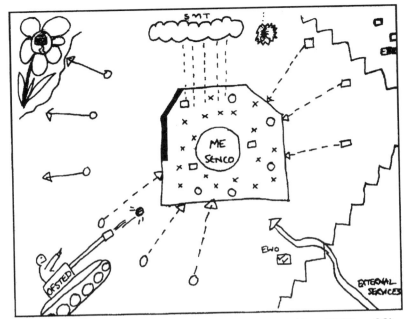

Figure 8.4   Concept map A (from Davies, Garner and Lee, 1999, p. 38).

Compare your ideas with the explanations that the people themselves give below.

 SENCO Sally's explanation of Figure 8.4:

I am in the middle – that's how I see it – surrounded by my children (these are the crosses), the teachers who really support me (they're the circles), the co-operative parents (the squares). I see this definitely as a little empire. It's not something I have set out to do, but I've had to do it to survive ... the thick black line in the drawing represents the barrier between me and some other teachers ... who seem out of date and at least one of them can't wait to leave ... The senior management team are often in a cloud because of lots of external pressures, like league tables and things not connected with the internal working of the school. Sometimes they are unable to stop the pressures getting through to me, so that's where the rain seeps in! ... The only support agency I feel I have an effective relationship with is the educational social worker, other services are too 'distant' to be of any use ... I drew OFSTED as a tank firing a cannonball ... The pastoral peace and quiet in the top left-hand corner is my home, where I can retire to lick my wounds, begin to feel optimistic again, stroke the cat and get ready to begin another day.

(Davies, Garner and Lee, 1999, p. 38)

*Figure 8.5   Concept map B (from Davies, Garner and Lee, 1999, p. 39).*

SENCO Chris's explanation of Figure 8.5:

Chris is a newly appointed SENCO and the role has senior management team status. Her drawing reflects her optimism and enthusiasm in her new post.

> I'm on 'cloud nine' because I'm doing something that's valuable and that those who work with me realize is very important to them. I have drawn a square in which I have drawn my classroom because it doesn't matter how things develop as far as my senior management post goes, I'll always see my first love as the children in my own class. I'm trying not to think about the Ofsted inspection next year so I've separated it off from me with barbed wire. My picture shows me juggling with seven or eight areas of SENCO work. I know it's going to be difficult at times, because more experienced teachers have told me this. I think that, at certain times, I simply won't be able to cope with all of the things required. This is why I show some things falling on to the floor. As far as I'm concerned, being a SENCO is about making decisions about what can and

can't be achieved in reality. There's no point in trying to do everything in the Code. What I shall do is to see what things are most important to my school and then try to fit them into my work pattern.

*(Davies, Garner and Lee, 1999, p. 39)*

Since this course explores developing perspectives in inclusive education, no examination of the SENCO perspective would be complete without a discussion as to whether the very existence of the post is in itself a barrier to inclusion. Is there any place for a role devoted to special educational needs in an inclusive school, where breadth of learning diversity is key rather than special educational need?

A critical issue within this debate is whether the requirements of legislation and of the Code of Practice and its implementation through special educational needs teams is keeping alive the role of the SENCO. Roaf regards the transmission of SENCO expertise to colleagues as an important step towards change. Equipping other colleagues to meet pupils' learning requirements enables SENCOs to concentrate on promoting inclusive education at whole school level through staff development and evaluation. As such, their traditional role would be replaced by one better described as 'inclusion manager' or 'learning support co-ordinator'. One SENCO, Pauline, gives voice to this perspective: 'I've asked to be called the Learning Support Co-ordinator now, it doesn't really fit, being a SENCO, in an inclusive school!' (Clough and Nutbrown, 2002, p. 4).

## Learning supporters

People who support pupils in classrooms are given different names in different areas. Learning support assistant, teaching assistant, classroom assistant, non-teaching assistant, special support assistant and educational assistant are widely used. Linda Shaw's term 'learning supporter' avoids the concept of 'assistant' being used to undermine the distinct characteristics of the role and its professional status:

There is a strong lobby for support work to be regarded in its own right, having its own intrinsic worth and making its own distinct contribution to children's learning. Supporters see their work as of equal value and complimentary to teachers' work and they want to be regarded as part of a team with teachers and other professionals to support pupils.

*(Shaw, 2001, p. 8)*

As school staff who spend the majority of their time supporting 'included pupils', their perspective on inclusion is an important one and we would support John O'Brien's claim (CSIE, 2002) that they have a critical contribution to make to educational debates about inclusion. Some of you may be learning supporters yourselves and have pertinent views on the subject – and what you would like to be called.

For those of you who are not learning supporters, a little background information may be helpful. Learning supporters are personnel based in schools. They form a very diverse group with differing levels of training and experience. Some have no formal qualifications and others are qualified teachers who have chosen the role rather than teaching.

Learning supporters are employed in a variety of different roles. They may be assigned to an individual pupil, to a small group of pupils, to general classroom support or to modification of teaching materials to facilitate greater pupil independence and inclusion. Some learning supporters work alongside pupils in the classroom, others withdraw the pupils for specialist input. Some only work with pupils on curriculum support, others have duties which include general classroom assistance – display work, preparation of art materials and so on. In some authorities these two roles are separated into two different posts – classroom assistants providing general assistance to the teacher (more common in infant classes) and learning supporters working exclusively on curricular/pupil support. Typical tasks include assisting pupils with scribing, or accessing, interpreting and organizing information. In addition, learning supporters are constantly motivating and reinforcing pupils and helping them manage their behaviour. The following quotations are from learning supporters describing their work:

> 'I am there to help pupils access information and make sure they understand it.'
>
> ...
>
> 'We help children to have an inclusive education and learn alongside their peers.'
>
> 'We build relationships with pupils and interact with many others on their behalf. Pupils don't really get much of a say. We are their feedback.'
>
> 'It is building up their self-esteem which will enable them to access education. The link between self-esteem and learning is so important.'
>
> *(quoted in Shaw, 2001, p. 7)*

Assisting better understanding of, and access to, the curriculum is a skilled process. Learning supporters need to understand the material themselves and enable the pupils to make connections with it. Indeed, in secondary schools, the specialist knowledge required means that learning supporters are often assigned to departments so that they can build up expertise in specific subjects.

*Learning supporters: mediators between the teacher, the children and the curriculum.*

## Conflicts and tensions

Many learning supporters feel that the move towards inclusion has made their role more complex without a matching increase in pay and status. Their average pay is often just above the minimum wage, they are frequently paid hourly, and in Roger Hancock *et al.*'s study (2002) only half were on permanent contracts. Maggie Balshaw's (1999) study revealed similar frustrations, the most common being employment on a series of temporary contracts, being thrown in at the deep end and not knowing teachers' expectations.

Learning supporters are usually funded out of individual schools' budgets. Fluctuating pupil numbers and some dependence on LEA funding for children with statements means that the need for learning supporters can change each term, so that many learning supporters are low-paid and have neither permanent contracts nor job security:

> We are paid similar to dinner ladies but look at what we have to do. And we don't know whether we are going to have jobs from one year to another. I was told I was appreciated in school but I am not valued enough for my job to be made permanent. It makes you feel very insecure. We want to do our best, we are extremely dedicated people, and we are being treated badly because of it.

*(quoted in Shaw, 2001, p. 13)*

Christina Tilstone draws attention to tensions in balancing the roles and responsibilities of teachers and learning supporters:

> There is a fine line to be drawn between exploiting this group of staff and properly involving them in the pupils' learning. It is not right to expect them to plan (especially as the lesson is in progress), produce resources, evaluate and record progress for the pupils they work with. Neither is it right for teachers to do all this for them without consulting, expecting them to carry out their plans without question. There needs to be a balance between the two.
>
> *(Tilstone et al., 2000, p. 61)*

Another source of tension occurs where learning supporters are required to work with pupils in ways they regard as exclusionary. For example a situation can arise where a pupil is 'nominally included' by being bodily present in a classroom, but 'attached' to a learning supporter in the corner of that classroom working in one-to-one isolation. Learning supporters also describe situations where pupils whose behaviour challenges experience 'inclusive seclusion' when, because they are regarded as too disruptive for other pupils, and they experience their learning in a separate room, again in one-to-one isolation with a learning supporter.

## ◯ Activity 8.8

Now read Chapter 19 in Reader 1, 'Learning support assistants talk about inclusion', by Caroline Roaf.

As you read the chapter, identify ways in which the assistants see themselves as supporting inclusion. Make notes of your thoughts on these questions in your learning journal.

The LSAs describe themselves as mediators between the class teacher, the child and the curriculum. They see themselves as an essential element of inclusive education, although they differ in their views of inclusion. Who they are in the community, and the social behaviour that they model, appears to help communication between the child and the school.

The need for training is a current theme in the literature, particularly in relation to collaborative team work. Gary Thomas (1992) draws a comparison between the amount of time and effort devoted to effective team work in industry compared to the paltry attention it is given in education. And yet it is essential that teachers and learning supporters develop an effective working relationship, collaborating and planning how their respective roles can best benefit their pupils. Shaw's research highlighted learning supporters' concerns about working relationships with teachers:

> 'Teachers don't always understand our role.
> They think it's useful to have an extra pair of hands.
> But what we are aiming for is how to get an effective learning situation.'

> 'In one class you might be treated as an equal and in the next considered only as a helper.'

> 'This isn't about keeping the teacher happy.
> It's about enlightening teachers about ways of helping themselves to help the child and for the child to be included that way.'
>
> *(Shaw, 2001, p. 11)*

Currently, most learning supporters get some basic induction training and there are various specialist courses available – some with accredited training – although learning supporters depend on the ability and willingness of individual schools to fund this training.

## Evolving responsibilities

The role of the learning supporter has been changing rapidly. Since the Code of Practice was revised in 2001 (DfES, 2001), SENCOs have increased their use of learning supporters to help them monitor and record pupil progress and implement IEPs. Where learning supporters might once have designed and adapted curricula for pupils, teachers are more likely to take responsibility for differentiating the curriculum and asking learning supporters to work towards particular targets and attainment levels with their pupils. The introduction of literacy and numeracy hours in England resulted in more ability grouping in classes and more learning supporters being used in a 'teaching' role. Initiatives to develop LSAs' teaching role have met with resistance but as an LSA comments: 'Please do not put down the role of LSAs, in this day and age we do not simply wash paint pots and wipe snotty noses!' (DfES, 2002).

Learning supporters should be sensitive to the need to strike the delicate balance between support and over-dependence. For example, the constant presence of an adult may interfere with normal peer-group interaction and affect pupils' ability to form relationships with other children. The learning supporter is presented with the dilemma of trying to support a pupil's learning whilst also trying to enable them to become more independent both educationally and socially.

Penny Lacey (2001) found wide disparities in the amount of responsibility held by LSAs. She describes some of the difficulties faced by learning supporters in these circumstances:

- lack of time and opportunity to talk and plan with the teacher;
- ambiguity in their role;
- teachers sometimes felt threatened by the learning supporter role;
- lack of resources and space;
- inadequate knowledge and experience;
- too much responsibility for the pay/status;
- teachers' inability to differentiate for pupils with severe learning difficulties;
- being left to get on with it without any help or guidance.

## Rewards and job satisfaction

Despite all the difficulties, low pay and frustrations, research indicates that learning supporters really do enjoy their work (Farrell *et al.*, 1999). Shaw collected learning supporters' comments about some of the satisfying aspects of their work. Here are a few of them for you to reflect on:

> 'Every time he completes his task it makes me happy.'
>
> 'Making a cricket game accessible to a severely disabled child.'
>
> 'Working with a group, including pupils experiencing difficulties, to rehearse and perform a short drama for assembly.
> All went well with great appreciation from the audience.'
>
> 'A young child with cerebral palsy who I work with has settled in brilliantly.
> There are no barriers to what he can and cannot do.
> This child's mother was told to put him in a special needs school, which I am grateful to say she refused to do.'
>
> 'All day in my work Chris gives me enjoyment and pride – when he talks and plays with friends, when he eats in the dining hall.
> All these are major steps to a life in society.'
>
> *(quoted in Shaw, 2001, p. 10)*

A striking feature of all the interviews with learning supporters in mainstream schools was their enthusiasm for the work they do. Almost without exception they stated that they felt that they were making a genuine contribution. They also felt that staff, parents and pupils valued their work. In particular they valued the opportunity to get to know a relatively small number of pupils really well, much more than a class teacher normally does.

We acknowledge that, like inclusion itself, our perspectives on inclusion are still evolving. Our own perspectives as writers of this course are changing as we constantly re-examine our own positions on inclusion. The quotation below is an example of how one learning supporter reappraised her orientation towards inclusion after her school started using the *Index for Inclusion* (Booth *et al.*, 2000):

> I never thought about some of the dimensions as being part of inclusive practice. I realize how inclusive we are! Of parents, of children from minority ethnic groups – It made me think – 'Am I being inclusive – as a professional?' Yes – I've really learned quite a bit – about me and my own attitudes ...
>
> *(Clough and Nutbrown, 2002, p. 3)*

## Headteachers

The part played by a headteacher in an inclusive school is vital in terms of leadership and high expectations. They are central to the construction of teams, the grouping of pupils and the encouraging of collaborative working practices. They can be inclusion ambassadors in their networking with other schools and agencies. They also have key roles in allocating funding and managing time to facilitate joint discussion, planning and evaluating amongst staff team members.

> Inclusion has to happen in everything we say and do. It can't just be added on ... It is about how you organize ordinary things like assemblies and lunch times, access to equipment, furniture, basic things, on one level. Then on the next level you say, 'What do we do to create a climate whereby everybody is accepted and valued?' That will include doing things like positive self-esteem and circle time, and co-operative collaborative learning, and discipline which is about relationships and not conflict.
>
> ... With principles, you have to set up quite a clear vision of the school so that everyone can have a clear view too. So we make it very clear to parents that any child is admitted. And staff were recruited on that principle as well. It was not something we surprised them with on their first day.
>
> *(quoted in Alderson, 1999, p. 44)*

Crucially, supportive headteachers can create a climate where teachers feel secure enough to take risks as they experiment with curricular adaptations and teaching styles in order to meet the challenges of diversity in their classrooms. Headteachers can also lead the way towards introducing more meaningful assessment procedures such as pupil profiling and records of achievement where pupils are measured in the context of their own diversity.

Headteachers continually face conflicts and tensions with regard to inclusion. They express concern about the emphasis on league tables and crude performance indicators:

The uncomfortable question has to be: if we became less successful and attracted fewer pupils, would this tempt us to become more selective, remove disruptive pupils or even direct money away from the classroom to spend on marketing the school?

*(quoted in Conway and Lawrence, 1992, p. 191).*

Pupils who are likely to do poorly in national tests may become unwelcome since their results affect schools' performance and positions in league tables. Schools are in direct competition with one another for pupil numbers and funding. Hence a vicious circle is created. Schools need to attract pupils in order to secure good levels of funding. Parents want a 'successful' school and often study league tables as part of choosing a school. This puts pressure on headteachers to exclude disruptive or low-scoring pupils and adopt strategies that they believe will achieve high academic grades, such as ability grouping. Some headteachers even fear that a good reputation for meeting the needs of all learners, including those with disabilities, may disadvantage them in the market place.

Helen Currie is the headteacher of the Thames Valley Consortium Traveller Education Service in Berkshire. She regards Gypsy Traveller children as one of the minority ethnic groups most at risk of exclusion. '... the Government appears to have shifted its priorities for Traveller children from access (social inclusion) to achievement (school improvement), with no recognition of the complexities of the interplay of mobility and ethnicity' (Currie and Danaher, 2001, p. 34). For example, Elizabeth Jordan (2001) maintains that full-time schooling is a barrier to children learning to be successful Travellers and therefore a threat to the very maintenance of their communities.

The emphasis on standardized testing has pushed the focus of those dealing with Traveller children onto achievement rather than curricular access. Furthermore, schools' anxiety about their positions in league tables has fuelled growing resistance to the admission of Traveller children.

## Activity 8.9

Chris Forlin (2001) examined teacher stress in relation to inclusion. In the box overleaf is a summary of the seven most and seven least stressful issues Forlin identified from 571 completed questionnaires. Imagine you are a headteacher in an inclusive school and you have just been handed these data. Study the data and jot down what you can learn from them and some ideas of the action you might take.

Teachers answered using a scale of 1 to 4, 1 = not stressful, 2 = somewhat stressful, 3 = quite stressful and 4 = extremely stressful.

*Most stressful*

| | |
|---|---|
| Reduced ability to teach other children effectively | 2.74 |
| Being held accountable for the child's educational outcomes | 2.58 |
| The child physically attacks others, e.g. hits or bites | 2.53 |
| Sustaining an active learning environment for the child | 2.53 |
| Difficulty in monitoring other students when attending to the child | 2.51 |
| The child disturbs other children | 2.49 |
| Time available for other students is reduced | 2.49 |

*Least stressful*

| | |
|---|---|
| Parents in the classroom | 1.44 |
| Obtaining relevant information about the child | 1.49 |
| Empathizing with parents | 1.50 |
| Parent/teacher tension | 1.54 |
| Limited contact with parents | 1.56 |
| Administering medication | 1.58 |
| Excessive meetings with parents | 1.61 |

*(adapted from Forlin, 2001, p. 240)*

# 4 Conclusion

In this unit we have begun to explore the curricular and pedagogical bases on which inclusion is built, with particular reference to the perspectives of different professionals. We return to this theme when we address making inclusion happen inside classrooms in Unit 13. We have highlighted the need for collaboration and team work and we explore this further in Unit 11. For professionals working in education, the drive for inclusion can result in tension and conflict as they wrestle with the practical challenges of putting inclusive theory into practice. As we saw at Bangabandhu School, however, working towards inclusive practice is a challenge best met through a positive approach.

# References

Alderson, P. (ed.) (1999) *Learning and Inclusion: the Cleves School experience*, London, David Fulton.

Appiah, L, (2000) 'Race and school exclusions: can the curriculum make a difference?', *Urban Education.* **18**(3), pp. 11–15.

Balshaw, M. H. (1999) *Help in the Classroom*, London: David Fulton.

Booth, T., Ainscow, M., Black-Hawkins, K., Vaughan, M. and Shaw, L. (2000) *Index for Inclusion: developing learning and participation in schools*, Bristol, CSIE.

Brownlee, J. and Carrington, S. (2000) 'Opportunities for authentic experience and reflection: a teaching programme designed to change attitudes towards disability for pre-service teachers', *Support for Learning*, **15**(3), pp. 99–105.

Bruce, T. (1991) *Early Childhood Education*, London, Hodder and Stoughton.

Bruner, J. (1977) 'Early social interaction and language acquisition' in Schaffer, H. R. (ed.) *Studies in Mother–Infant Interaction*, London, Academic Press.

Bruner, J. (1985) 'Vygotsky: a historical and conceptual perspective' in Wertsch, J. V. (ed.) *Culture, Communication and Cognition: Vygotskian perspectives*, New York, Cambridge University Press.

Bruner, J. (1993) 'Readiness for learning' in Anglin, J. (ed.) *Beyond the Information Given*, New York, W. W. Norton.

Centre for Studies on Inclusive Education (CSIE) (2002) 'Learning supporters and inclusion: next steps forward: report of national conferences in London and Manchester', on line at: http://inclusion.uwe.ac.uk/csie/lsaconfreport.htm [accessed November 2003].

Clough, P. (1999) 'Exclusive tendencies: concepts, consciousness and curriculum in the project of inclusion', *International Journal of Inclusive Education*, **3**(1), pp. 63–73.

Clough, P. and Nutbrown, C. (2002) 'The *Index for Inclusion*: personal perspectives from early years educators', *Early Education*, Spring 2002.

Conway, J. and Lawrence, M. (1992) 'Competition between schools: inclusion or exclusion?' in Potts, P., Armstrong, F. and Masterton, M. (eds) *Equality and Diversity in Education Volume 1: learning, teaching and managing schools*, London, Routledge in association with The Open University, pp. 185–91.

Corbett, J. (2001) *Supporting Inclusive Education: a connective pedagogy*, London, RoutledgeFalmer.

Currie, H. and Danaher, P. A. (2001) 'Government funding for English Traveller education support services', *Multicultural Teaching*, **19**(2), pp. 33–6.

Davies, J. D., Garner, P. and Lee, J. (1999) 'Special educational needs co-ordinators and the Code: no longer practising', *Support for Learning*, **14**(1), pp. 37–40.

Department for Education and Employment (DfEE) (2001) *Supporting the Target Setting Process* (DfEE/0065/2001), London, DfEE.

Department for Education and Skills (DfES) (2002) Message posted by Cindy on 'Education in the news', discussion forum on The Standards Site. Available at: http://www.standards.dfes.gov.uk/forums/ showflat.pl?Board=education&Number=703 [accessed November 2003].

Department for Education and Skills (DfES) (2003) *Disapplication of the National Curriculum (Revised)*, London, DfES. Available from: http://www.dfes.gov.uk/disapply/pdfs/1990_Guidance.pdf [accessed November 2003].

Diller, D. (1999) 'Opening the dialogue: using culture as a tool in teaching young African-American children', *The Reading Teacher*, **52**(8), pp. 820–27.

Donaldson, M. (1978) *Children's Minds*, London, Fonatana/Collins.

Dyson, A. (2000) 'Questioning, understanding and supporting the inclusive school' in Daniels, H. (ed.) *Special Education Reformed: beyond rhetoric?* London, Falmer Press.

Farrell, P. (1997) *Teaching Pupils with Learning Difficulties*, London, Cassell.

Farrell, P., Balshaw, M. and Polat, F. (1999) *The Management, Role and Training of Learning Support Assistants*, London, DfEE.

Forlin, C. (2001) 'Inclusion: identifying potential stressors for regular class teachers', *Educational Research*, **43**(3), pp. 235–45.

Garner, P. (2000) 'Teachers' and pupils' voices on inclusion: preferred strategies for children who are regarded as having emotional and behavioural difficulties (EBD)', paper presented at International Special Education Congress 2000. Available at: http://www.isec2000.org.uk/abstracts/papers_g/garner_2.htm [accessed February 2003].

Gerland , G. (1997) 'A real person', *Communication*, Spring, pp. 15–116.

Hancock, R., Swann, W., Marr, A., and Turner, J. (2001) 'Classroom assistants in primary schools: employment and deployment', ESRC research project R000237803, summary on line at: http://www.regard.ac.uk/research_findings/R000237803/summary.pdf [accessed November 2003].

Hornby, G. and Kidd, R. (2001) 'Transfer from special to mainstream – ten years later', *British Journal of Special Education*, **28**(1), pp. 10–17.

Jenkinson, J. (1997) *Mainstream or Special? Educating students with disabilities*, London, Routledge.

Jordan, E. (2001) 'Interrupted learning: the Traveller paradigm', *Support for Learning*, **16**(3), pp. 128–34.

Keefe, C. H. (1996) *Label-Free Learning: supporting learners with disabilities*, Portland (Maine), Stenhouse Publishers.

Kellett, M. (1998) 'An exploratory study of ways to enhance young children's listening skills and raise self esteem', unpublished MA(Ed) thesis, Oxford, Oxford Brookes University.

Lacey, P. (2001) 'The role of learning support assistants in the inclusive learning of pupils with severe and profound learning difficulties', *Educational Review*, **53**(2), pp. 157–67.

Lee, L. (1962) *Cider with Rosie*, Harmondsworth, Penguin Books.

Lewis, A. with Norwich, B. (2000) 'Mapping pedagogy for special educational needs', paper presented at International Special Education Congress 2000.

Light, P. H., Buckingham, N. and Robbins, H. (1979) 'The development of communication: competence as a function of age', *Child Development* **40**, pp. 255–66.

McGarvey, B., Marriott, S., Morgan V. and Abbott, L. (1998) 'Approaches to differentiation in the core subjects: the experience of Northern Ireland primary teachers', *Evaluation and Research in Education*, **12**(3), pp. 140–52.

McKenzie, J. (1998) 'The WIRED classroom: How are the students engaged?', *From Now On. The Educational Technology Journal*, **7**(6). Available from: http://fno.org/mar98/flotilla2.html [accessed July 2002].

Mittler, P. (2000) *Working towards Inclusive Education: social contexts*, London, David Fulton.

O'Brien, T. (1998) 'The millennium curriculum: confronting the issues and proposing solutions', *Support for Learning*, **13**(4), pp. 147–52.

O'Donoghue, T. A. and Chalmers, R. (2000) 'How teachers manage their work in inclusive classrooms', *Teaching and Teacher Education*, **16**, pp. 889–904.

Piaget, J. and Inhelder, B. (1972) (trans. Weaver, H.) *The Psychology of the Child*, New York: Basic Books.

Pollard, A. and Bourne, J. (eds) (1994) *Teaching and Learning in the Primary School*, London, Cassell.

Reeves, T. (1997) 'Evaluating what really matters in computer-based education' in *Learning with Software: pedagogies and practice*, Australian Education Department and Open Learning Technology Corporation Limited website, available from: http://www.educationau.edu.au/archives/cp/reeves.htm [accessed November 2003].

Rix, J. (2002) '3 stage progressive differentiation – an approach to the problems faced when implementing communicative language methods within mainstream schools', unpublished MA thesis, London, King's College, University of London.

Roaf, C. (1998) 'Inclusion, the Code of Practice and the role of the SENCO' in Clough, P. (ed.) *Managing Inclusive Education: from policy to practice*, London, Paul Chapman, pp. 114–29.

Rose, R. (2001) 'Primary school teacher perceptions of the conditions required to include pupils with special educational needs', *Educational Review*, **53**(2), pp. 147–56.

Roth, I. (2002) 'Working with the autistic spectrum: from theory to practice' in Brace, N. and Westcott, H. (eds) *Applying Psychology*, Book 3 of DSE 212 *Exploring Psychology*, Milton Keynes, The Open University, pp. 243–370.

School Curriculum and Assessment Authority (SCAA) (1994) *The Review of the National Curriculum: a report on the 1994 consultation*, London, SCAA.

Scruggs, T. E. and Mastropieri, M. A. (1996) 'Teacher perceptions of mainstreaming/inclusion, 1958–1995: a research synthesis', *Exceptional Children*, **63**, pp. 59–74.

Shaw, L. (2001) *Learning Supporters and Inclusion*, Bristol, Centre for Studies on Inclusive Education.

Sheehy, K. (2000) 'The development of cognition, moral reasoning and language' in Gupta, D. and Gupta, R. (eds) *Psychology for Psychiatrists*, London, Whurr.

Sheehy, K. (2002) 'The effective use of symbols in teaching word recognition to children with severe learning difficulties: a comparison of word alone, integrated picture cueing and the handle technique', *International Journal of Disability, Development and Education*, **49**(1), pp. 47–59.

Social Exclusion Unit (SEU) (1998) *Truancy and School Exclusion*, London, SEU.

Thomas, G. (1992) *Effective Classroom Teamwork: support or intrusion?*, London: Routledge.

Thomas, G. and Loxley, A. (2001) *Deconstructing Special Education and Constructing Inclusion*, Buckingham: Open University Press.

Thomas, G., Walker, D. and Webb, J. (1998) *The Making of the Inclusive School*, London: Routledge.

Tilstone, C., Lacey, P., Porter, J. and Robertson, C. (2000) *Pupils with Learning Difficulties in Mainstream Schools*, London, David Fulton.

Udvari-Solner, A. and Thousand, J. (1995) 'Effective organizational, instructional and curricular practices in inclusive schools and classrooms' in Clark, C., Dyson, A. and Millward, A. (eds) *Towards Inclusive Schools?*, London, David Fulton.

# Acknowledgements

Grateful acknowledgement is made to the following for permission to reproduce material in this book.

## Unit 5

*Figure 5.1*: Crown copyright material is reproduced under Class Licence Number C010000065 with the permission of the Controller of HMSO and the Queen's Printer for Scotland.

The Course Team would like to thank the staff and pupils of Bangabandhu Primary School for all their help during the production of Unit 5.

## Unit 6

### Text

Appendix 1: Centre for Studies on Inclusive Education.

### Illustrations

Pages 57 and 58: Alliance for Inclusive Education.

## Unit 7

### Figures

*Figure 7.1*: Froese, P. *et al.* (1999) 'Comparing opinions of people with developmental disabilities and significant persons in their lives using the individual supports identification system', Disability and Society, **14**(6), Taylor and Francis; *Figure 7.2*: Carter, C. and Osler, A. (2000) 'Human rights, identities and conflict management: a study of school culture as experienced through classroom relationships', *Cambridge Journal of Education*, **30**(3), Taylor and Francis.

### Illustrations

*Pages 101 and 104*: courtesy of Down's Syndrome Association; *pages 109, 115, 116 and 123*: © Sally &Richard Greenhill.

## Unit 8

### Figures

*Figure 8.2*: Schoolsnet (www.schoolsnet.com); *Figure 8.3*: adapted from the work of Kath Sayer in Thomas, G. and Loxley, A. (2001) *Deconstructing Special Education and Constructing Inclusion*, Open University Press; *Figure 8.4*: Davies, J. D., Garner, P. and Lee, J. (1999) 'Special educational needs coordinators and the code: no longer practising', Support for Learning, **14**(1), pp. 37-40.

## Illustrations

*Page 164*: David Walsh.